REVE...

JESUS CHRIST'...

SELECT STUDIES FROM THE A...

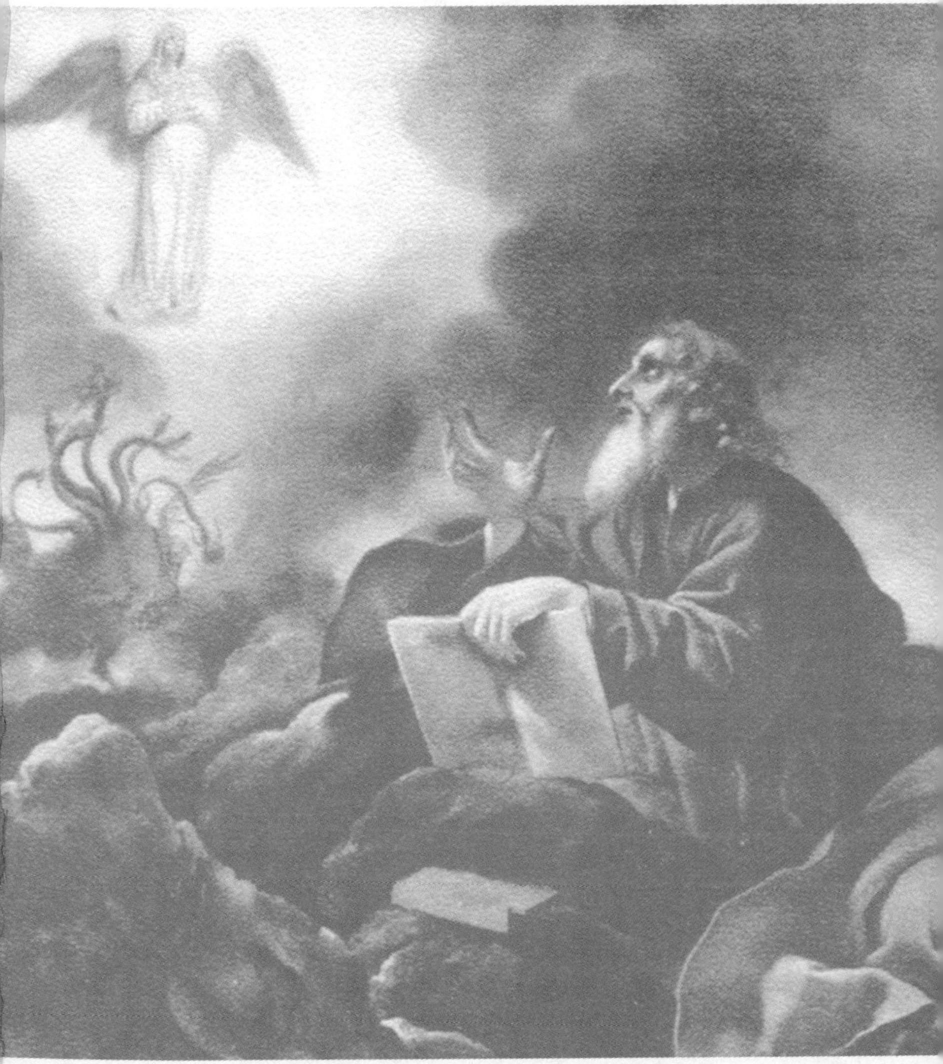

WAYNE JACKSON

REVELATION: JESUS CHRIST'S LAST MESSAGE OF HOPE –
SELECT STUDIES FROM THE APOCALYPSE

© 2004 by Courier Publications, Inc.

All rights reserved. No part of this book may be reproduced in any form without written permission of the publisher except in the case of brief quotations embodied in critical articles or reviews.

ISBN: 1-932723-01-3

Additional copies may be ordered from:

Courier Publications
7809 N. Pershing Avenue
Stockton, CA 95207

http://www.christiancourier.com
http://www.courierpublications.com

PREFACE

Despite the flippant attitude of some, who can zip through the book of Revelation in an hour or so and tell you all about it, the final book of the Bible unquestionably is the most difficult treatise in the inspired collection of New Testament literature. A few have found the narrative so baffling they dismissed it altogether. In 1522, Martin Luther declared: "My spirit cannot adjust itself to the book [of Revelation]." Luther rejected the divine origin of the Apocalypse.

In spite of some enigmatic sections, there are still numerous wonderful and practical truths that can be gleaned from the holy record by the average Bible student. These are precious gems that lift the discouraged spirit and nudge the saint toward his heavenly home.

This volume is not intended to be a verse-by-verse commentary on Revelation. Rather, it represents a study of various themes that are found within the sacred pages. Additionally, the author has attempted to address some of the fanciful errors that have arisen in "Christendom" as a result of a failure to understand the symbolic nature of the document.

The reader may not agree with every conclusion the author has drawn. All one can ask is that a fair hearing be granted to the evidence presented. It is hoped that, at the very least, a greater appreciation for the richness and value of Revelation will be generated.

My appreciation is extended to Jared Jackson for his technical production expertise, and to David Boggs and Brandon Renfroe for their labor proofing the final manuscript.

WAYNE JACKSON

TABLE OF CONTENTS

Introduction *1*

CHAPTER 1

An Introduction to the Book of Revelation *3*

CHAPTER 2

Word Patterns in the Book of Revelation *15*

CHAPTER 3

John on the Isle of Patmos *27*

CHAPTER 4

The Letters to the Seven Churches *33*

CHAPTER 5

Visions of the Throne of God *39*

CHAPTER 6

Souls Under the Altar of God *47*

CHAPTER 7

Who Are the One Hundred Forty-four Thousand? *55*

CHAPTER 8

The Mark of the Beast (Part 1) *59*

CHAPTER 9

The Mark of the Beast (Part 2) *65*

CHAPTER 10
> The Mark of the Beast (Part 3) 77

CHAPTER 11
> The Battle of Armageddon 85

CHAPTER 12
> The Thousand-Year Reign of Christ 93

CHAPTER 13
> A New Heavens and A New Earth 109

APPENDIX I
> Does Revelation Sanction the Doctrine of "The Rapture"? . . .117

APPENDIX II
> Who is Paul's "Man of Sin"? 121

APPENDIX III
> The Time is "At Hand" 135

APPENDIX IV
> When Was the Book of Revelation Written? 141

APPENDIX V
> Jesus Christ: The First and The Last 149

APPENDIX VI
> Marginal Notes from the Book of Revelation 153

> Bibliographic Sources 227

INTRODUCTION

In 1995, I published a book entitled, **Select Studies in the Book of Revelation**. It has been an immensely popular volume, having gone through a number of reprints since that time. It has been used as a class study, for sermon preparation, and for devotional enjoyment. We have been grateful for the enthusiastic response.

This latest edition has been expanded and retitled, **Revelation: Jesus Christ's Last Message of Hope – Select Studies from the Apocalypse**. This change reflects the increase in content: this version contains almost twice the amount of information than the initial production.

In addition to the thirteen chapters and three appendices contained in the original edition, the present book has two additional appendices: "When Was the Book of Revelation Written?" and "Jesus Christ: The First and The Last." The dating of John's book is especially significant inasmuch as a major false doctrine – that of realized eschatology, known also as "the A.D. 70 Doctrine" – depends upon a *pre*-A.D. 70 date for the book. One prominent leader in the "realized" movement has conceded that if the book of Revelation was composed *after* the fall of Jerusalem (A.D. 70), their entire theory crashes. This chapter, therefore, examines the evidence for the case that Revelation was written in the mid-90's A.D., and not before the destruction of Jerusalem.

More significantly, in this edition we have added a sizable section of "notes" on certain select passages – from every chapter in the book. The format follows that of our popular book, **Notes From the Margin of My Bible**. These "notes" provide the student with some of the rich treasures to be mined from the sacred document. Some have suggested that this additional section alone is worth the price of the book.

And so, with thanksgiving to God, and to his servant, John who endured the hardships of Patmos, we send forth this expanded effort, **Revelation: Jesus Christ's Last Message of Hope – Select Studies from the Apocalypse,** with the fond hope that it will bless many for years yet to come.

CHAPTER 1

AN INTRODUCTION TO THE BOOK OF REVELATION

In spite of the fact that we are encouraged to read and to keep the things written in the book of Revelation (1:3; 22:7), many still entertain the notion that this composition is beyond the grasp of the average Christian. While it is true that the book is not without its difficulties – due to the nature of its symbolic language – still, the general thrust can be apprehended. In addition, many important truths and practical lessons abound within this divine document.

The Author

The writer calls himself "John" (1:1, 4, 9; 22:8), and casts himself in the role of an inspired prophet (1:10, 11; 22:9). The earliest patristic traditions (e.g., Justin Martyr, Irenaeus, Clement of Alexandria, Tertullian, and Origen) identify this "John" as the son of Zebedee, the Lord's apostle. It was not until the late third century A.D. (Eusebius) that the apostle's authorship of the narrative was questioned. But "who, in the first century, would venture to call himself simply John, in the living presence, or recent memory, of so dominating a figure as the last surviving apostle?" (Blaiklock, p. 247). The critical arguments against the apostle's authorship are highly subjective and poorly grounded.

The Date and Destination

Most scholars believe that John wrote the Revelation from the island of Patmos (1:9) – in the Aegean Sea about fifty-six miles southwest of Ephesus – during the reign of the emperor Domitian (A.D. 81-96). Ancient testimony (Irenaeus, Clement of Alexandria, Victorinus, Eusebius, etc.) is virtually unanimous in this conviction (see Jackson, 1989, pp. 25, 26).

The book was primarily addressed to seven congregations in the Roman province of Asia (1:4, 11). There were other churches in this area, but these seven appear to be *representative* of the problems and needs of the congregations of that region. Clearly, the book is designed to encourage the Lord's people in all ages.

Style and Purpose

The book of Revelation is a form of literature styled "apocalyptic," which means that it is characterized by a series of visions which are portrayed in *symbolic* language (cf. 1:1). In spite of the fact that some deny it (McGuiggan, p. 15), this type of writing was common in times of great danger (which is clearly evidenced in this book). It was employed to "smuggle" a message of hope to the Lord's people, when an unambiguous declaration of victory would have multiplied their afflictions.

Significantly, the signs of the book are largely borrowed from the Old Testament which, of course, would be familiar to the saints. Of the 404 verses in Revelation, some 265 contain references from the Old Testament, involving approximately 550 Old Testament passages (Smith, 1963, p. 1495).

The basic design of the book is to show that, in spite of the devastating persecution to which Christians were being – and would be – subjected, the cause of Jesus Christ would ultimately be victorious over all opposing forces. The key word in Revelation is "overcome" (cf. 2:7, 11, 17, 26; 3:5, 12, 21). Christ has "overcome" (5:5), and so shall his people.

Attempts to literalize the figures of this book have resulted in much confusion. Examples of this are seen in the "Watchtower Witness" claim that only 144,000 will enter heaven (7:4; 14:1), and the millennialists' belief in a literal 1,000-year earthly reign of Christ (20:1-8).

Schools of Interpretation

Due to the difficult symbols of the book, it is not surprising that there is considerable variance of opinion as to the interpretation of the specifics of John's message. The major schools of thought in approaching the book of Revelation are principally four – with some variation even within these different groups.

The Preterist View

The term "preterist" denotes "that which has gone by," and, generally, this approach argues that the book has to do with a series of calamities that occurred during the early times of the church. Manley says that this view is "adopted by the Roman church, and at the other extreme by the rationalistic critics" (p. 412). That charge is a bit too general. There are several subdivisions within the Preterist camp.

The Liberal View

Liberalism, with its so-called historical-critical approach, alleges that John was predicting the fall of Rome and the end of the world in the rather immediate future, but that he was mistaken. This theory rejects the concept of Bible inspiration.

Realized Eschatology

This is the notion that all Bible prophecy – including the second coming of Christ, the resurrection of the dead, the judgment day, and the end of the world (which events are spiritualized) – were fulfilled by the time Jerusalem was destroyed in A.D. 70. It is without any semblance of scriptural support (see Jackson, 1990a).

Early Preterism

This concept has the book of Revelation dealing primarily with the Jewish and Neronian persecutions of the primitive church. It sees the book as being written in the late 60's and substantially fulfilled by A.D. 70. Foy E. Wallace, Jr. advocated this position. This view, however, is negated by the strong evidence that the book was not written until a quarter of a century *after* A.D. 70. Hendriksen says: "We have not found a single, really cogent argument in support of the earlier date" (p. 19).

Late Preterism

Advocates of this idea see the Apocalypse as being mostly fulfilled when Constantine legalized Christianity (A.D. 313), or by the time Rome fell (A.D. 476), thus stemming the tide of Roman oppression. J.W. Roberts argued this viewpoint in the Sweet commentary series, and so has Jim McGuiggan; it is a very popular position today among those of a conservative persuasion. Many who advocate this view appear to be unaware of the fact that it was conceived initially by a Catholic priest.

A weakness of this concept, however, is that it fails to recognize the correlation of Revelation with other prophetic literature (e.g., Daniel). Further, it implies that the final New Testament book totally ignores that great apostasy from the faith, which is so clearly prophesied elsewhere in the New Testament (cf. 2 Thes. 2:1ff; 1 Tim. 4:1ff). This force became a church-state organism that viciously persecuted those attempting to practice primitive Christianity.

Another major flaw in the preterist theory is that "the decisive victory portrayed in the latter chapters of the Apocalypse was never achieved" with any proximity to the fall of Rome (Mounce, pp. 41, 42).

The Futurist View

This theory alleges that most of the book of Revelation is as yet unfulfilled. Chapters four through twenty-two supposedly pertain to events associated with the second coming of Christ, and so are still believed to be future (Thiessen, 1943, p. 326). This concept, characterized by extreme literalism (e.g., an actual 1,000-year earthly reign of Christ) is the view of premillennialists and dispensationalists. Since this theory is grounded in the unscriptural system of millennialism, it obviously is erroneous.

The Idealist View

The Idealist View of the book of Revelation suggests that the document is unrelated to specific historical events; rather, the symbols merely deal with the ongoing struggle between the church and her foes, whoever they may be, throughout Christian history. This concept, however, ignores the book's claim that it contains actual prophecy (1:3; 22:7, 10-19), which was to commence (though not conclude) its fulfillment in the near future (1:1-3, 19).

The Historical View

The Historical View of Revelation was commonly held by the Protestant reformers, and also the leaders of the early restoration movement. It contends that the Apocalypse deals with prophecies which find fulfillment in actual events of history – and that such fulfillment extends beyond the era of the Roman empire.

While there is disagreement among the advocates of this view as to the interpretation of many details, there is general concurrence that the Revelation pictures the victory of the church of Jesus Christ over pagan Rome. Beyond this, though, there would be triumph of God's people over the oppression of that apostate ecclesiastical movement which grew out of, and received considerable support from, civil Rome. This concept is set forth in John T. Hinds' commentary in the Gospel Advocate series (see also the works of Elliott, Barnes, Clarke, and Alford – to mention a few).

Several objections are advanced against this view. First, in order to understand the book, it is said, one would have to know church history. But doesn't one have to know *something* of history to appreciate the fulfillment of *any* prophecy? Who could possibly appreciate the significance of Daniel 2 without a knowledge of the history of those empires that succeeded the Babylonian regime?

Second, if the visions were centuries in their fulfillment, what relevance could this have had for the early Christians? The answer is – the same sort of relevance that the Messianic hope had for the Old Testament saints.

Third, it is claimed that since there is much disagreement among expositors as to the historical identification of the symbols, this concept must not be correct. This is not a logical objection. This line of reasoning would negate confidence on practically any biblical topic. Disagreement over some details of interpretation does not vitiate a general proposition regarding the book as a whole.

The Plan of the Book

The way one outlines the book of Revelation will depend, to some extent, upon the interpretive view that he assumes regarding the document as a whole. The following scheme has proved helpful to the author.

1. The Introduction and Inaugural Vision (1:1-20).
2. The Letters to the Seven Congregations of Asia (2, 3).
3. Visions of the Heavenly Throne and the Lamb (4, 5).
4. Visions of Christian Victory – Part I (6:1-11:18).
5. Visions of Christian Victory – Part II (11:19-20:15).
6. The Final State (21:1-22:5).
7. Concluding Warnings and Exhortations (22:6-21).

Great Lessons in the Book

Regardless of any disagreements sincere people may entertain regarding the specific historical application of the book of Revelation, there are numerous theological propositions clearly affirmed in the record. A variety of admonitions are quite helpful to those who explore the treasures of this document.

God

There are great affirmations in this book regarding God. He is the eternal God of the past, present, and future (1:4; 4:9). He is the Almighty (1:8). God is called the "Almighty" ten times in the New Testament – nine of these instances are in Revelation. God is our Creator (4:11; 14:7) who is worthy of the adoration of the entire creation because of his infinite holiness (4:8). Before him men will ultimately stand for judgment (20:11-15).

Christ

Revelation overflows with declarations regarding the nature of the Son of God. His earthly historicity is acknowledged – an offspring of David, from the tribe of Judah (5:5), and yet, he is as eternal as the Father (22:13; cf. 1:8; see also 1 Tim. 6:16), and thus is divine, as well as human (2:18; cf. 19:13 with John 1:1); little wonder that he is an object of worship (5:8-14). He was involved with Jehovah as Creator of the universe (3:14; cf. 1 Cor. 8:6; Heb. 1:2). Jesus was put to death by crucifixion (11:8), and in that capacity He was the Lamb of God by whom the price for sin was paid (1:5; 5:9).

Christ is designated as a "lamb" twenty-seven times in the Apocalypse (c.f. 5:8, 12, 13). But he was raised from the dead (1:5) and is alive for evermore (1:18). He functions as prophet (1:1), king (1:5), and even the garment of his visionary appearance was reminiscent of a priest (1:13; cf. Ex. 28:4). Finally, Christ will return to render judgment and punish those who have stood against truth (19:11-16).

Victory

As mentioned earlier, this book signals the ultimate *victory* of God's people. The Greek word *nikao* means: to conquer, to overcome, to gain victory. The term is found twenty-eight times in the New Testament, and seventeen of these are in Revelation. Christ overcame by virtue of his death and resurrection (3:21; 5:5), and ultimately will be victorious over all his enemies (17:14).

As a consequence of Jesus' death, the victory of Christians is anticipated as well (12:11, 12). The letters to the churches of Asia make it clear, however; the conquest is conditional – saints must be faithful if they would overcome. Those who continue to overcome (the verbs are present tense, denoting sustained activity) are promised that they will: eat of the tree of life (2:7); not be hurt of the second death (2:11); be given hidden manna and a white stone on which a new name was inscribed (2:17) – all symbols of victory (Barclay, 1957, pp. 53, 54); be given authority over the nations (2:26) and granted the morning star (2:28; cf. 22:16); be arrayed in white garments with their names in the book of life and confessed before the Father (3:5); be made a pillar in God's temple, find security, and be given a new name (3:12); and, join Christ in victory (3:21).

The Blessedness of Obedience

In times of persecution, there is a temptation to abandon the faith and take the path of least resistance. The Apocalypse pronounces a blessedness upon those who maintain fidelity. Note these "beatitudes" in the book. Blessed are those who: read, hear, and keep the words of this book (1:3; 22:7); die in the Lord (14:13); watch, and keep their garments (16:15); are bidden to the Lamb's marriage supper (19:9); have part in the first resurrection (20:6); and, wash their garments (22:14; cf. 7:14).

The Final State of the Righteous

The final glory of the Lord's people is characterized in both a negative and positive fashion in this book. The negative aspect is emphasized by a series of "no-mores." There will be *no more:* going out (3:12) – a suggestion of an eternal abiding place where there is no failure (Plumptre, p. 185); hunger, thirst, or scorching heat (7:16); Babylon, the captor of God's people (18:21-23); material earth and sea (21:1; cf. Mt. 24:35); death, mourning, crying, or pain (21:4); and, no more curse, such as was imposed in Eden (22:3). During the symbolic 1,000 years, Satan's power to completely deceive exists no more (20:3). There is much hope in the "no-more" sections. The saints' ultimate triumph is also frequently represented under the descriptive of something "new." The Greek word *kainos*, which denotes qualitative newness, or freshness, is found eight times in this book. Mention is made of a new name (2:17; 3:12), the new Jerusalem (3:12; 21:2), a new song (5:9; 14:3), a new heaven and a new earth (21:1) – indeed, all things are to be made new (21:5).

The Destiny of the Wicked

Inasmuch as the final book of the Bible predicts the victory of the righteous over their enemies, it is not at all strange that the same document would address the issue of the destiny of those who have arrayed themselves against the Almighty, and who stand in opposition to his Lamb. There is, therefore, considerable information in Revelation regarding the punishment of the wicked.

When Christ returns, His enemies will "mourn" in view of their anticipated judgment (1:7). God's opponents will be subjected to "the second death" (2:11; 20:14; 21:8), which is the ultimate separation from God (cf. 2 Thes. 1:9).

Satanic forces will be victims of a divine war (2:16; 19:11), in which they will be crushed like fragile pottery (2:27). They will be recipients of sacred wrath – represented by two different Greek words, *thumos* (nine times - 14:8; 15:1; 19:15, etc.) and *orge* (six times; 6:16, 17; 16:19; 19:15, etc.). The ungodly will be tormented (14:10; 20:10), with no rest forever (14:11), in the crushing winepress of Heaven's justice (14:19; 19:15), even in everlasting fire (19:20; 20:14, 15; 21:8).

Conclusion

The book of Revelation is a fascinating and profitable treatise. It should be explored more frequently. But it must be studied with care. Its message, conveyed in vivid and dramatic imagery, must ever find harmony with the more lucid portions of the biblical record.

CHAPTER 2

WORD PATTERNS IN THE BOOK OF REVELATION

In his wilderness confrontation with Satan, Jesus declared: "Man shall not live by bread alone, but by every word that proceeds out of the mouth of God" (Mt. 4:4). Where are those "words," which man must consume, if he would obtain the life that is eternal? They are found in the Bible. Christ plainly stated: "[T]he words that I have spoken unto you are spirit, and are life" (Jn. 6:63). Later, Paul wrote that the "Scriptures" are inspired of God (2 Tim. 3:16).

The term "Scriptures" denotes "that which has been written," and in the Bible it is always employed of a divine writing. The Holy Scriptures are thus composed of "words." These words are those which the Holy Spirit guided the writers in using as they wrote by sacred inspiration (cf. Mt. 10:19; Jn. 14:26; 16:13). The study of biblical words is very important.

Etymology

Words may be examined in various ways. Frequently it is profitable to explore the etymology of a word. The term "Comforter" (Jn. 14:26) translates the Greek word *parakletos*, from *para*, "beside," and *kaleo*, "to call." Etymologically, it suggests the idea of an aid called to one's side for the purpose of encouraging, exhorting, consoling, or defending that individual (cf. Vine, p. 142).

Grammatical Form

Additionally, words should be examined in terms of their grammatical form. In the case of a verb, for example, such matters as tense, voice, and mood are of great significance. The tense indicates the type of action under consideration (time takes a secondary place). Voice has to do with the speaker's relationship to the action (e.g., is he acting, or being acted upon?). And mood reveals the speaker's disposition relative to the action (e.g., is he stating a fact, or commanding a response?).

Context

The context is the ultimate consideration for determining the significance of a word in a particular setting. Context can override etymology; context can create a situation in which normal grammatical principles are set aside (for example, a present tense form may be used in prophecy to emphasize the certainty of an event's fulfillment; cf. Mt. 3:10).

Pattern of Usage

Another way that words can be studied is by examining their pattern of usage in a particular narrative. If, for example, one notices that a certain word appears to be rather randomly dispersed throughout the New Testament books, and then he discovers a concentration of that term in a certain section of scripture, he may wonder if the word has taken on a special emphasis for that biblical writer. There are certain "word patterns" that appear in the book of Revelation. Let us reflect upon some of these.

Overcome

As indicated in Chapter 1, one of the important words in the Apocalypse – if not the key term – is the Greek word *nikao*, which is rendered by English expressions such as "overcome," "prevail," "conquer," and "victory." The base form is found twenty-eight times in the New Testament, and seventeen of these are in Revelation. Obviously, there is significance to this word pattern.

Three times *nikao* is used of human rulers. The military success of the Roman empire is depicted under the symbol of a rider on a white horse, a "conquering" force (6:2) – hinting of the oppression that Christianity would have to endure. A persecuting "beast" would make war against the saints "overcoming" them (11:7; 13:7), but the victory is only temporary. Ultimately, the Lamb, and those who identify with his cause, are the victors.

Nikao is employed of Christ several times. Jesus overcame and sat down on his Father's throne (3:21). His victory qualified him to open the prophetic seals which revealed the impending events of history (5:5). And even though hostile forces assault him, the Lamb will overcome these enemies for he is King of kings and Lord of lords (17:14).

Finally, *nikao* is used repeatedly of the victory that saints shall enjoy as a result of their sustained fidelity to the Son of God (see 2:7, 11, 17, 26; 3:5, 12, 21; 12:11; 15:2; 21:7). There is victory for Christians on account of the victory of the Lamb (12:11; 17:14).

Seven

"Seven" (Grk. *hepta*) takes on special significance in this book. Of the eighty-eight times it is found in the New Testament, fifty-six of these are in Revelation. "Seven" is employed to suggest *completeness, fullness, or inclusiveness.*

The expression "seven Spirits" (1:4; 3:1; 4:5) suggests the completeness of the Holy Spirit's work. The "seven lampstands" signify the seven congregations of Asia, and the "seven stars" are the messengers representing these churches (1:20). Seven congregations and messengers are selected because they perfectly illustrate the challenges and needs of the Lord's people in that day (or any day).

The mysterious scroll of chapter six is sealed with "seven seals," which may indicate that the document was "absolutely" validated (Jones, p. 27), or perhaps the seven seals hint of the "fullness" of the historical revelation about to be unfolded.

Christ is described as having "seven horns," symbolizing his perfect power and authority, while the "seven eyes" of the Lamb may point to the Savior's omniscience (cf. Zech. 4:10), as well as his cooperative labor with the Holy Spirit (5:6).

"Seven angels" represent a complete company of heavenly servants, ready to do the bidding of God Almighty, and the "seven trumpets" which they have depict the perfect judgments of Jehovah, which are to be visited upon the earth (8:2).

The "seven thunders" later mentioned suggest a similar idea (10:3). Likewise "seven plagues" (15:1), and "seven bowls of wrath" (15:7; 16:1ff) suggest the thoroughness of divine punishment upon the Lamb's foes.

White

"White" is used as a frequent symbol in Revelation. The Greek term *leukos* occurs approximately twenty-six times in the New Testament – sixteen of these in the last book. Depending upon the context, the adjective can suggest "victory" or "purity." The "white horse" suggests success in conquest; it is used of a Roman force in 6:2, and later, of the final victory of Christ at the Judgment (19:11).

The whiteness of the Lord's "hair" (1:14) likely suggested honor, dignity (cf. Lev. 19:32; Prov. 16:31) or purity (Dan.

7:9). The "white throne" upon which the Judge ⟨...⟩ sits (20:11) may convey the idea of its gleaming b⟨...⟩ so underscores the authority and majesty of him wh⟨...⟩ ⟨...⟩es it (Mounce, p 364). The fact that Christ is sitting on a "white cloud" (14:14) indicates that he is victorious over death, and has been crowned king.

White "robes" or "garments" are common figures in this book. The symbol may suggest the *pure* character of the one who is so adorned. The twenty-four elders at God's throne were arrayed in white garments (4:4). The Lord counsels the church in Laodicea to obtain white garments that their shame may be covered (3:18). The great multitude standing before Christ, clad in white apparel (7:9), represented those who cleansed their robes in the blood of the Lamb (7:13, 14). The Lord's heavenly army is adorned in clothes that are white and pure (19:14).

On the other hand, as mentioned above, "white" can sometimes reflect the concept of victory. Those in Sardis who do not defile their garments (i.e., corrupt themselves with false religion or moral degeneration), Christ promises, "shall [future tense] walk with me in white" (3:4).

In Pergamum, the Lord vows that those who overcome will be given a "white stone" (2:17). The "stone" may refer to the manner of jury voting – a white stone affirming innocence. It would thus be a symbol of vindication – the world may find you guilty, but I will pronounce you vindicated!

Almighty

The Greek word *pantokrator* derives from two roots – *pan*, "all," and *krateo*, "to hold." It thus suggests one who holds all things or persons within his grasp. The word is used but ten times in the entire New Testament, and nine of these instances are in Revelation (1:8; 4:8; 11:17; 15:3; 16:7, 14; 19:6, 15; 21:22) – the solitary exception is 2 Corinthians 6:18.

As those early Christians faced death for the cause of Jesus, they might easily have wondered: Is God really in control? Inspiration wishes to calm the hearts of troubled saints. The Almighty holds all things within his hand. No matter how dismal circumstances may appear, a time of reckoning is coming; it will be at the "great day of God, the Almighty" (16:14). What a word of consolation! Very meaningful – then and now.

Throne

The English word "throne" is a transliteration of the Greek *thronos*, a word suggesting dignity, power, or a seat of authority. Of the sixty-two times that *thronos* is found in the New Testament, forty-seven of these (76%) are in the Apocalypse.

The influence of the devil in the city of Pergamum is stressed by suggesting that this is where "Satan's throne" dwells (2:13). Pergamum was an ancient concentration of false worship. It was a center for the worship of Asklepios, the "god of healing." The city also contained shrines for the worship of Zeus and Athene. Perhaps more importantly, Pergamum was a major city of Caesar worship. Clearly, Satan exercised great sway in this community (see Barclay, 1957, pp. 42-46). The powerful influence of the persecuting "beast" is described as a "throne" granted by Satan (13:2), but later a divine bowl of God's wrath is poured out on the devil's throne, and his kingdom is darkened (16:10).

Jesus promised that all who overcome will sit down with him on his throne (i.e., share his regal glory), even as he overcame and sat down with his Father (3:21). This passage cannot be harmonized with the notion that Christ will not reign until the alleged "millennial" era. Moreover, even though Christ, at the end, will deliver his mediatorial reign back to God (1 Cor. 15:24-28), nevertheless, he will share a royal splendor with the Father throughout eternity (22:1).

Jehovah's heavenly authority is frequently symbolized as a "throne" in Revelation (4:2ff; 5:1ff; 6:16; 7:9ff, etc.). Though the twenty-four elders around his throne possess delegated authority (4:4), they acknowledge the supreme rule of God (4:10). In 20:11, the "white throne" is that of the final Judgment.

In an environment where it must have appeared that Satan and his henchmen were occupying the thrones of power, the Lord Jesus wants his people to know that such, in fact, is not the case. Deity still rules, in spite of how the temporary scene seems. This is a great word of comfort for the oppressed.

Crown

The Greek New Testament has two words for "crown." The first is *stephanos*, the victory crown – a symbol of triumph – presented, for instance, to the winner of a race. *Stephanos* is found eighteen times in the New Testament, and eight of these are in the last book. Those who remain faithful, even if death is the cost, will receive the "crown of life" (2:10); care must be exercised, however, that no one "take your crown" (i.e., rob you of your victory – 3:11). Can a child of God fall from grace? Certainly.

Triumph of powers is suggested by the crown in some passages. The assault of certain political powers, under the permission of God, is represented under the term "crown" (6:2; 9:7). The church, under the figure of a woman, is crowned with twelve stars (12:1), probably symbolic of the Lord's apostles, leaders (inspired luminaries) representing the Savior's authority (cf. 21:14). The crown hints of the church's victory over the dragon.

In 14:14-16, John sees one "like unto a son of man" (cf. 1:13) sitting on a white cloud, and wearing a "golden crown." He comes forth with a sharp sickle and the harvest is effected. Most commentators see this as a reference to Christ, the crown being emblematic of the fact that the Son of Man has conquered and thus has the right to render judgment (Mounce, p. 279) – though a few would argue that this being is a mere angel (Morris, p. 184). The weight of the evidence is with the former view.

The other Greek term for "crown" is *diadem*. *Diadem* occurs only three times in the New Testament, and all of these are in Revelation. *Diadem* is the crown of royalty. The dragon (Satan) who persecutes the woman (church) is described as having *diadems* on his seven heads (12:3), probably suggesting the devil's *claim* to regal authority (cf. Mt. 4:8, 9), and his extraordinary power over his subjects. The beast (pagan Rome) that ascends from the sea (13:1), also is adorned with ten *diadems* – likely with the same import as suggested of the dragon. Finally, the divine Christ, who comes to render judgment, is arrayed with "many *diadems*" (19:12). The Messiah is vastly superior to his enemies, and will destroy them all.

Lamb

The Greek Testament contains two words for "lamb." *Amnos* is found four times (Jn. 1:29, 36; Acts 8:32; 1 Pet. 1:19). Each of these passages figuratively designate Christ as being in some fashion like a lamb.

The other word, *arnion*, is employed twenty-nine times in the New Testament, and twenty-eight of the occurrences are in Revelation. John 21:15 is the exception. "Lamb" is the most common designation for Christ in the final book of the Bible.

Notice these characteristics of the Messianic Lamb:

(1) The Lamb has been slain (5:6, 9, 12; 13:8), but he is

"standing" (5:6) (i.e., raised from the dead), and he is alive for evermore (1:18).

(2) The Lamb is the *leader* of his people (7:17; 14:1-4). Strikingly, 7:17 has Jesus represented as both a lamb and a shepherd.

(3) The Lamb is the redeemer and the owner of his international kingdom (5:9, 10; 14:4), and the husband of his spiritual wife (19:7-9). The Lamb is also a judge whose anger against evil will be revealed in the Great Day of God (6:16; 14:10).

Beasts

The word "beasts" is common in the English translation of the Bible – even more so in the King James Version, than in other translations. The term *zoon* (twenty-three times in the New Testament; twenty times in Revelation) merely denotes "a living creature." It is used exclusively of "the four living creatures" who stand before the throne of God and give glory, honor, and thanks to the Lord (cf. 4:8, 9), and who perfectly serve him (cf. 5:14; 6:1-7). It is inappropriate to render it as "beasts" in Revelation, in view of the negative connotation of that term (Vine, p. 67).

Therion is also translated as "beast," but it is a "wild beast." The word occurs forty-six times in the New Testament, thirty-nine of which are in Revelation. In the Apocalypse, *therion* signifies two malignant creatures which represent determined enemies of Almighty God and his holy cause. Many scholars believe these beasts are symbolic of pagan Rome, and later, papal Rome (see chapters 8, 9, and 10 – "The Mark of the Beast.")

Horses

The horse (*hippos*) is mentioned sixteen times in the New Testament. Fifteen of these are in the book of Revelation (the other reference is James 3:3). The obvious reason for the employment of the horse-symbol in the Apocalypse is the Old Testament background which emphasizes the use of this magnificent animal as an instrument of war. In fact, of the some 150 references to horses in the Bible, approximately ninety occurrences are figurative or prophetic in character (Richards, p. 497).

Old Testament law forbade Israel to "multiply horses" (Deut. 17:14-16), because the horse was a war machine, and the people of God needed to learn to trust in their Creator, rather than their own military prowess (cf. Psa. 33:17; Ezek. 17:15).

In Revelation, the horse becomes a symbol of hostile, persecuting forces against Christianity (cf. 6:2-8), or providential instruments for the punishment of evil men (9:7ff). Additionally, as this grand document draws toward its conclusion, the Lord Jesus is seen victoriously riding a white horse in the battle which will see his enemies destroyed (19:11). His faithful servants also follow him on white horses (19:14), suggesting that they partake of the triumph accomplished by the Son of God.

For Ever and Ever

Sometimes the word "forever" figuratively denotes a limited period of time (cf. Ex. 12:14). However, when the expression "for ever and ever" is used in the New Testament, it always suggests that which is unending in duration. This phrase is found nineteen times in the New Testament, and thirteen of these are in Revelation. Both the Father and the Son live for ever and ever (1:18; 4:10; 10:6; 15:7), and are worthy of glory, dominion, etc., for ever and ever (1:6; 4:9; 5:13; 7:12). Both the Lord and his people will reign for ever and ever (11:15; 22:5), but God's enemies will be defeated and punished for ever and ever (14:11; 19:3; 20:10).

The word patterns within the book of Revelation are significant indeed. We do not pretend to have exhausted this theme. This does, however, present some exciting challenges for continued study.

CHAPTER 3

JOHN ON THE ISLE OF PATMOS

This magnificent book opens with the affirmation that the narrative contains the "Revelation of Jesus Christ" (1:1). The expression can mean either a revelation from Christ, or a revelation about him. Both ideas are true; likely, though, the former is the thrust of this passage. Be that as it may, the message is one to be conveyed to the apostle by an angel who was to be involved in the presentation of a series of visions (note the word "saw" in verse 2 – a concept stressed frequently in the book). The truths would be couched in symbolic language (as suggested by "signified" – vs. 1), hence, as indicated in our introductory chapter, it is a serious mistake to literalize the word pictures of this volume. At the conclusion of the initial paragraph, a blessing is pronounced upon those who hear the words of this document and who keep it. Surely this must indicate that the book was designed to be understood. While there may be considerable difficulty in interpreting some of the symbols in this inspired treatise, countless practical lessons are easily discernible.

The final book of the New Testament is a book of prophecy (1:3). And it deals with events which are to commence their fulfillment in those waning days of the first century. John writes concerning the things "which must shortly come to pass" (1:1), and he says "for the time is at hand" (1:3). This does not mean that the entire series of visions are to be imminently fulfilled, as some allege; rather, a series of historical events are about to *start* unfolding, which will ultimately be consummated at the end of the world by the great victory achieved by the Lamb of God (see

Appendix III, "The Time is 'At Hand'"). As we mentioned before, "victory" is the theme of the Apocalypse.

The book is primarily addressed to seven congregations of the church of Christ in the Roman province of Asia Minor. Ultimately, of course, it is for the benefit of Christians across the centuries. These seven churches are selected most likely because they are representative of the problems and challenges facing the body of Christ as a whole – both then and now.

The Salutation

In the Salutation of the book (1:4-8), there is a greeting from the divine Godhead – him who was, is, and is to come (the Father), the seven spirits before his throne (an allusion to the Holy Spirit – "seven" denoting the completeness of his revelatory function; cf. 3:1; 4:5; 5:6), and from Jesus Christ. The Lord Jesus is described in a number of remarkable ways. He is the "faithful and true witness," an expression validating the integrity of his message. Jesus is the "firstborn" of the dead. The term denotes the sovereignty he possesses by virtue of his resurrection (cf. Psa. 89:27; Col. 1:18) He thus is the "ruler of the kings of the earth." That is an affirmation that would be quite meaningful to these saints who are suffering at the hands of evil civil rulers.

Next, the redemptive work of the Lord is detailed. He loves (note the present tense form – suggesting a continuous love) us, and he loosed us from our sins by his blood. The past tense verb looks back to Calvary. John makes it very clear – without the sacrificial death of Christ, there would be no forgiveness of sin. That blood is applied, of course, when we enter the church, which the Lord's blood purchased (Acts 20:28), and we enter the church when we culminate our initial obedience by being immersed into the body of Christ (1 Cor. 12:13).

Finally, what we are permitted to become, as a result of Jesus' mission, is set forth. We are his "kingdom." It is folly to deny that the Lord's kingdom has already come, as do the millennialists. We were translated into the Lord's kingdom by virtue of our response to the new birth process (Jn. 3:3-5; Col. 1:13). Additionally, all Christians are "priests" unto God (cf. 1 Pet. 2:5, 9). We are allowed to serve Jehovah in his temple (the church – 1 Cor. 3:16) by virtue of the work that our High Priest has accomplished already (Heb. 10:19ff). John closes his salutation by setting forth the promise of the Lord's glorious return. He will come victoriously, and his enemies will mourn. There is a hint of impending judgment. Authenticating the apostle's testimony is the word of the Almighty, eternal God himself (so signifies the expression "the Alpha and the Omega").

The Preparatory Vision

John has been banished to the desolate island of Patmos because he has proclaimed the word of God and the testimony of Jesus (see 1:2). He knows the plight of the persecuted saints; he is their kinsman in Christ, and a partaker with them in tribulation, endurance, and the kingdom of Christ (1:9).

It is the "Lord's day." This term denotes the first day of the week, Sunday. It is designated "the Lord's day" because on this day Christ was raised from the dead (Mt. 28:1; Mk. 16:1; Lk. 24:1; Jn. 20:1). This is a special time belonging to the Lord, and Christians have definite religious obligations on this day. When a person becomes a child of God, he needs to commit to this day as a time of worship – and never forsake it for frivolous reasons.

John was under the influence of the Spirit, and he is given a vision of the risen Son of God – a scene that is designed to prepare him for the great revelations which he will subsequently receive. This situation is not unfamiliar to the Bible student. In the Old Testament, both Isaiah (6:1ff) and Ezekiel (1:1ff) received similar preparatory visions.

The apostle heard a voice which sounded like a great trumpet. He was then instructed to write down a description of what he saw. About 140 times in this book, the reader is informed that John "saw" certain glorious scenes; a dozen times he is told to "write" these experiences. As John turns, he observes seven golden lampstands, which represent the seven congregations of Asia (1:20). In the "midst" of these lampstands was one "like unto a son of man" – a common appellation in other New Testament documents for Jesus Christ (cf. Mt. 8:20; Mk. 2:10; Lk. 19:10; Jn. 3:13). The clothing of this divine being is reminiscent of the Old Testament high priest (cf. Ex. 28:4) – a clear suggestion of the priesthood of Christ. It is interesting that Jesus is described in this chapter with terms which suggest that he is our prophet (1:1), priest (1:13), and king (1:5).

The Son of man appears with hair that is white as wool – a description of God in the Old Testament (Dan. 7:9). His eyes were penetrating, like flames of fire (cf. 2:18; 19:12). His feet were like burnished brass – perhaps suggesting he had walked the earth in purity, and his voice sounded like many waters. This last descriptive is also a suggestion of his divine nature (see Ezek. 43:2).

In his right hand, he held seven stars, which we are later told represent seven messengers of the seven churches (1:20). Who are these messengers? We are not told. Possibly they were representatives from the seven congregations who had been appointed to minister to John on barren Patmos, and to convey messages from the apostle to those saints (cf. 2:1, etc.). At any rate, the point clearly is made that the Lord is aware of what is transpiring in these churches, and their destiny is in his hand – regardless of the threats of the pagan hostilities. Out of the Lord's mouth proceeded a sharp, two-edged sword, clearly representative of his word (cf. Heb. 4:12), by which men will be judged ultimately (Jn. 12:48; 2 Thes. 2:8). His appearance was like the brightness of the sun in its zenith. One cannot but be reminded of the transfiguration scene when the Lord's divine nature shown forth in all its radiance (Mt. 17:2).

When John witnessed this scene, he was virtually paralyzed. He fell as one dead at the Master's feet (1:17). But Jesus admonished: "Fear not" – literally: "Stop being afraid." More than once, in years gone by, the compassionate Christ had lifted the spirits of his fearful disciples (cf. Mt. 14:27; 17:7; Acts 27:24). Jesus then affirmed several important truths regarding himself (1:17, 18). Note these:

(1) "I am the first and the last." This expression is an affirmation of eternal existence. It is employed in conjunction with "Alpha and Omega" in 22:13, which designation is applied to God himself in 1:8 (See Appendix V).

(2) Christ is the "Living one." The present tense participle form suggests that he is the *always* Living one – both past, present, and future. Of whom could that be said except deity?

(3) Though he was put to death, now he is "alive for evermore" – a fact acknowledged by the heavenly beings in the great throne-room scene (cf. 4:9).

(4) Finally, the Lord says: "I have the keys of death and Hades." "Death" refers to the disposition of the *body* at the time of its demise. "Hades" is an allusion to the receptacle of the *spirit* at the time of death. There are several important points to be noted here.

First, it suggests that by the power of his own resurrection, Christ eventually will raise the dead and unite new, spiritual bodies with those disembodied souls. The persecuting forces may kill the saints, but Jesus holds the "keys" (power to open) which will rectify that circumstance.

Second, this implies that there is a difference between the body and the spirit (cf. Mt. 10:28; Jas. 2:26); it denies the doctrine of materialism.

Third, it reveals that "Hades" was not emptied at the time of the Lord's ascension, as some allege.

At the conclusion of this enthralling vision, John is charged once more to "write" (1:19) He is instructed to write: (a) the things which he saw; (b) the things which are; and, (c) the things which shall come to pass hereafter. Some scholars see this as almost a rough outline of the book. The "things which you [he] saw" is alleged to be a reference to the vision of Patmos. The "things which are" are perceived as a description of the conditions of the seven congregations, as addressed in chapters 2 and 3. And the "things which shall come to pass hereafter" are viewed as the prophetic revelations made known in chapters 4ff. This does not suggest, of course, that they all are *still* future from our *present* vantage point – as millennialists contend.

Clearly, the initial chapter of the book of Revelation is crucial to the balance of the narrative. It sets the stage, in an awesome way, for the great scenes that are to follow. There are many uplifting truths to be gleaned from this opening portion of the Apocalypse, and certainly this chapter is not characterized by the difficulty that follows in some of the subsequent sections. Read and profit from it.

CHAPTER 4

THE LETTERS TO THE SEVEN CHURCHES

In preparation for those grand visions which would constitute the book of Revelation, the apostle John was confronted by the risen Christ on the island of Patmos. Jesus was said to be "in the midst" of the seven golden lampstands, which represented seven congregations of the Lord's body in Asia (1:13, 20). Later, Christ was characterized as "he who walks [present tense – constantly walks] among the seven golden lampstands" (2:1). Since the Lord ever moves among his people, one is not surprised to learn that he is intimately aware of what transpires within his churches. Accordingly, in the letters to the seven congregations, the Bible student is repeatedly reminded that the Son of God "knows" the nature of their circumstances (2:2, 9, 13, 19; 3:1, 8, 15). Based upon his perfect knowledge, Christ commended those qualities which were to be enhanced. Similarly, he addressed some changes to be effected, if heaven was to be finally obtained.

The epistles to the seven churches follow a general pattern of development. They contain: a *salutation* from the Lord; a *commendation* of virtues when justified; a *condemnation* of wrongs where such was needed; an *exhortation* to continued fidelity; and finally, a promise of *exaltation* to those who overcome. Some of the churches presented an exception to the pattern. For example, there was no rebuke for either Smyrna or Philadelphia; but, by way of contrast, Jesus had nothing good to say regarding Laodicea.

It is certainly reasonable to contend that whatever the Lord approved, or disapproved, in those ancient churches, he would similarly approve or disapprove in his congregations of today (cf. Heb. 13:8). Let us thus reflect upon these two broad categories.

Commendation

Christ praised a number of qualities characteristic of the church in Ephesus. These were Christians who had labored diligently – to the point of exhaustion, for so signifies the term *kopos*, "toil." Moreover, in spite of persecution, they had remained patient; i.e., they had endured the hostilities of the enemy with fidelity. Additionally, they were doctrinally sound; they had put to the test certain teachers who claimed to be apostles, but were not. Clearly, these brethren practiced church discipline. Finally, the Ephesians had persevered for the Lord's name sake, and they had not grown tired of serving the Master (2:2, 3).

Though the church in Smyrna had been subjected to severe persecution by those who feigned a relationship to Judaism, and though they were economically destitute (cf. Heb. 10:34), these saints were spiritually rich in their service to the Son of God (2:9). Clearly they were wealthy in good works (1 Tim. 6:18).

In Pergamum, the children of God held fast the Lord's name; they did not deny his faith even though one of their number had suffered martyrdom; they were a courageous group (2:13).

The church in Thyatira had several praise-worthy qualities. Unlike Ephesus, their love shown brightly, and that devotion expressed itself in service. Too, their faith (confidence, trust) was firm, and this allowed them to endure tribulation. Finally, these Christians had not simply "held their own" against their persecutors; actually, they had grown spiritually – their latter works were more than the first (2:19).

Sardis was mostly a tragedy. There was no word of general praise for this church. There is but a brief recognition that a few souls in this city had remained pure; they had not defiled their spiritual attire (3:4).

Though the church in Philadelphia had "little power," possibly suggesting it was small in number, the saints had faithfully kept the Lord's word, and had not denied his name. For this they were praised (3:8).

Condemnation

While Jesus was happy to render praise where praise was due, it is also a fact that he was compelled to rebuke church flaws as well. And from such descriptives we can learn the sort of attitudes and conduct that must be avoided. Again, we note that there was no word of censure for either Smyrna or Philadelphia – a remarkable commentary on the maturity of these two churches.

In spite of its commendable traits, the church at Ephesus had left its "first love," i.e., their devotion to God, and the benevolence for his people, that had characterized the earlier days of their congregational existence. Though active in many areas, their attitude was that of a "fallen" group. They were thus commanded to repent or else they would lose their identity as a church of Jesus Christ (2:4, 5).

The church at Pergamum was contaminated by some who held to the doctrine of Balaam, an Old Testament character who taught the pagan king Balak how to corrupt the Israelite people in the matter of participating in idolatry and the commission of fornication. Others endorsed the teaching of the Nicolaitans, who apparently held a "like manner" doctrine (2:14, 15). Repentance was demanded or else the Lord would come and make war with these rebels.

The congregation in the city of Thyatira was afflicted with a similar weakness. They were overlooking the evil teaching of a woman called "Jezebel" (doubtless a symbolic appellation for an evil woman who was reminiscent of the Israelite queen who corrupted Israel through her spineless husband). This "Jezebel" feigned being a prophetess, and through her teaching she led Christians into idolatry and sexual misconduct (2:20, 21). The Lord threatened to destroy those thus involved in order to demonstrate "to all the churches" that he knew of their depraved conduct and that he had the authority to judge them.

In Sardis, the situation was lamentable. Members of the body in this city had the reputation of being a very lively group. They were "on fire" for the Master. However, the Lord, who sees not as man (1 Sam. 16:7), knew that in reality they were spiritually dead. Too, this was a start-and-stop church. They were erratic, ever initiating projects, yet not bringing them to fruition. Christ therefore admonished them to "establish the things that remain," i.e., they were to stabilize themselves and proceed with doing God's will (3:2).

The church in Laodicea was a disaster and the members thereof were utterly oblivious to this fact. Though they boasted of their wealth, and took pride in their independence, the Lord saw them as wretched, miserable, poor, blind, and naked (3:17). The Laodicean congregation was lukewarm (3:16) – a condition that makes Christ sick. Their apathy was such that they had excluded the Son of God from their fellowship and he pled for reentry (3:20).

A consideration of the foregoing commendations and condemnations recorded in these seven epistles leads to the enlightening conclusion that our Lord Jesus Christ desires the following characteristics in his congregations:

- Churches that are obedient to his Word.
- Churches that are energetic.
- Churches that endure against opposition.
- Churches that are sound in doctrine.
- Churches that are tireless in their labor.
- Churches that are courageous in the face of death.
- Churches that are loving in disposition.
- Churches that are confident, trusting God.
- Churches that serve the needs of others.
- Churches that grow spiritually and numerically.
- Churches that are pure and penitent.
- Churches that refuse to tolerate false teaching.
- Churches that discipline wayward members.
- Churches that are zealous and stable.
- Churches that practice self-evaluation.
- Churches in which he is an abiding presence.

A careful consideration of both desirable and undesirable traits of these primitive churches can be of supreme value today. May God help us improve our congregations and strive for the divine model.

CHAPTER 5

VISIONS OF THE THRONE OF GOD

Chapters 4 and 5 of the book of Revelation are remarkable for what they reveal about God, the Father, and his blessed Son, Jesus Christ. The emphasis of chapter 4 is the majesty of God the Father. The Lamb is given prominence in chapter 5.

Praise to the Father

John records that he saw a door "opened" in heaven (4:1). The verbal form is a perfect tense, suggesting that the door opened and remained so – doubtless for John's benefit. This is strikingly similar to the way Ezekiel's visions commenced. "The heavens were opened, and I saw visions of God" (Ezek. 1:1). The apostle heard a voice bidding him to "come up hither" so that he may be shown "the things which must come to pass hereafter." Reflect upon the word "must" – it reveals that God is in charge of human history. This is a thought that would be very helpful to Christians in a time of persecution.

John was again said to be "in the Spirit" (4:2). He had been "in the spirit" earlier (1:10), and now returns to that state. This likely suggests that the visions of this book were received piecemeal, so that between them, the apostle assumed his normal status. He saw a throne set in heaven, and upon this throne was Almighty God (4:8). The throne symbolized the sovereignty of Jehovah. "God reigns over the nations; God sits upon his holy throne" (Psa. 47:8). It was (and is) important for saints to know that regardless of how adverse our physical circumstances appear to be, God is still in control!

We do not know the precise form God assumed as John saw him upon the throne. There was some resemblance to a human figure (cf. 5:1), although the language is certainly anthropomorphic (i.e., deity described in human form). The Creator appeared bathed in light "like a jasper stone and a sardius: and there was a rainbow round about the throne, like an emerald to look upon" (4:3). The ideas associated with these precious stones are difficult to identify – probably they are designed to highlight different aspects of the majestic nature of God who dwells in light unapproachable (1 Tim. 6:16).

The rainbow, of course, reminds us of the Flood in Noah's day (Gen. 9:16, 17) – a circumstance in which judgment and mercy were combined. And this is not a situation unknown to the theme of this book. Saints will be recipients of heaven's mercy; the enemy will receive divine judgment.

Around the throne of God were twenty-four thrones occupied by a corresponding number of "elders." Who are these elders? They probably denote an order of angelic beings. The word "elders" seems to be used in that sense in Isaiah 24:23, and these "elders" distinguish themselves from those who are purchased with the Lamb's blood, i.e., earthly saints, in the song recorded in 5:9, 10. Note the contrast between "them" and "our" in verse 10 (see Jones, p. 25; Mounce, p. 135).

The elders were arrayed in white, reflecting their purity. Upon their heads were crowns of gold. This suggests that they had been granted some sort of regal authority. Apparently there is an order of authority among angels (cf. Jude 6).

Out of God's throne came forth lightnings, voices, and thunders. These are demonstrations of the power and sovereignty of the Almighty (cf. Ex. 19:16ff; Psa. 18:12ff; 77:18). These scenes should impress us greatly with the magnificent nature of God.

Additionally, there were seven lamps burning (continuously). As suggested in connection with 1:4, we believe this to be a reference to the Holy Spirit. The numeral seven denotes the perfection of the Spirit's role as the revealer of divine truth (spiritual light), made known through the Holy Scriptures (2 Tim. 3:16, 17).

Before the Lord's throne there was, as it were, a "sea of glass" like crystal (4:6). One can only imagine how this sea reflected and magnified the brilliant qualities of God illustrated by the radiance mentioned earlier. Some view the "sea" as suggesting a separation between God and his creatures, thus stressing his holiness (Jones, p. 25). Or perhaps it is a symbol of victory – much like the Red Sea became a victory sign for Israel in the Old Testament (Roberts, p. 55). Maybe it hints of the calmness of those who are true worshipers of God (Hinds, p. 21; Morris p. 90). Obviously, ideas regarding this matter are diverse.

In proximity to the throne were "four living creatures" full of eyes before and behind. One was like a lion, another resembled a calf, the third had a face like a man, and the fourth was like a flying eagle. Each of them had six wings, were full of eyes round about and within, and they worshiped God continuously. Again, mystery surrounds the identity of these beings. Clearly they resemble the creatures in Ezekiel's vision (1:10; cf. 10:20). But what do they signify? Mounce suggests that the creatures represent "an exalted order of angelic beings" (p. 138; cf. Roberts, p. 56). Jones feels that they are distinguished from angels in 5:11. If that is so, then the twenty-four elders do not represent angels either. Is there some order of heavenly beings that is neither deity, angelic, or human? It seems impossible to say on the information available.

On the other hand, H.B. Swete speculated that the "four

forms suggest whatever is noblest, strongest, wisest, and swiftest in animate Nature. Nature, including Man, is represented before the Throne, taking its part in the fulfillment of the Divine Will, and the worship of the Divine Majesty" (as quoted by Morris, p. 91). This would simply suggest, in a highly symbolic manner, that Jehovah is worthy of worship by his entire creation. This is a possible view, yet the symbolic adoration of nature's creatures seems to be set apart from the living creatures in 5:11-14.

The living creatures were saying: "Holy, holy, holy, is the Lord God, the Almighty, who was and who is and who is to come." This parallels the praise of the seraphim in Isaiah's throne-room scene (6:1ff). In John's vision, these living ones extol the holiness, the might, and the eternality of the Creator. As the living creatures render glory, honor, and thanksgiving to the eternal God, the elders follow, casting down their crowns before the throne, obviously acknowledging the complete sovereignty of the Creator. Verse 11 clearly reflects that God is "worthy" of adoration because of his role as the Creator (cf. Psa. 18:3). In view of this, can we not see how wicked it is to deny the biblical doctrine of creation, and seek purely naturalistic explanations for the earth and its inhabitants?

Praise to the Lamb

As the inspired apostle observed the heavenly vision, he noticed that in the right hand (emphasizing importance) of the Almighty was a scroll, written on both sides. This hinted of the completeness of the message. It may have been composed of several pages, for it was sealed with seven seals. A strong angel, with a loud voice, asked: "Who is worthy [i.e., who had the *spiritual qualifications*] to open the book, and to loose the seals thereof?" No creature anywhere was suited for such a notable task.

Chapter 5: Visions of the Throne of God

Why not? Obviously because this was a scroll dealing with events to come; only a *divine being* would be capable of directing future earthly activity. What a commentary this is relative to Christ! When John contemplated the possibility that the scroll might remain sealed, he *audibly* wept much [so the original word indicates]. One of the twenty-four elders interrupted him: "Stop crying." He then explained. "Behold, the Lion that is of the tribe of Judah, the Root of David, hath overcome to open the scroll and the seven seals thereof" (5:5). There is much valuable information in this brief section.

First, the regal authority of Christ is suggested by the descriptive, "Lion" (cf. Gen. 49:9). Second, he was from the tribe of Judah. The Old Testament had foretold the coming of the Messiah out of the tribe of Judah (see Gen. 49:10; Heb. 7:14). Third, Jesus is the "Root of David." This is generally viewed as a reference to the fact that Christ was descended from the Davidic line. Normally, however, a "root" is the source from which the plant springs (cf. 1 Tim. 6:10). Moreover, in 22:16 Christ is both the "root" and the "offspring" of David – "root" seems thus to be something different from "offspring." Hiebert observes that 22:16 "denotes divine-human nature as the source and descendant of David" (p. 172). Fourth, Christ is said to have "overcome." The tense indicates that the event has already been achieved. The victory was won at Calvary – the rest is a mopping-up campaign!

As John surveyed this vision, he saw – in the midst of the throne, the living creatures, and the elders – a Lamb, standing, as though it had been slain. The word rendered "lamb" (*arnion*) is common in Revelation (see Chapter 2, "Word Patterns.") Although the Lamb appeared as though it had been slain, it was "standing" (the perfect tense form suggests that it stood up and remained standing!). The Lamb had seven horns. Since "horn" frequently symbolizes power (cf. Deut. 33:17) and, as "seven" denotes perfection, there is the suggestion here that the Lamb was perfect in might.

It has been significantly observed that no one but an inspired composer would have used the Lamb motif as a symbol for Christianity. Men employ ravenous beasts to represent their movements. The United States uses the eagle; Russia, the bear; Great Britain, the lion; France, the tiger. Only the kingdom of heaven would dare use the Lamb as a symbol of its might (see Morris, p. 96).

Too, the Lamb had "seven eyes," which represented the "seven Spirits of God" (i.e., the Holy Spirit; cf. 1:4). These were sent forth (perfect tense – hinting of the abiding nature of the mission) into all the earth. The Lamb's revelation is made known by the Holy Spirit (Jn. 14:16-18), hence, the Spirit is sometimes designated as the Spirit of Christ (cf. Acts 16:7; Gal. 4:6). The close association between the members of the Godhead is frequently indicated in the Scriptures.

The Lamb took the scroll from the right hand of the Creator. Note the cooperation between these divine Persons. What a signal event this must have been, for it evoked a magnificent response from the living creatures and the elders. They fell down before the Lamb. Can there be any stronger statement of the deity of the Lord Jesus Christ? Each of these heavenly creatures, prostrate before the Lamb, has both a harp and a golden bowl full of incense. The harps are symbols of praise, and the incense represents "the prayers of the saints" (Psa. 141:2; cf. Lk. 1:10). It is crass literalism to suggest that the mention of "harps" can serve as a justification for the use of mechanical instruments of music in Christian worship. If such an argument were valid, it would also sanction the burning of incense as an act of New Testament worship. Moreover, as John T. Hinds observed, if this context is to be viewed as a literal precedent for church worship, then each Christian would be required to play his own harp, "which is quite enough to show the absurdity of any such interpretation" (p. 80).

These heavenly creatures were singing a "new" [*kainos*, new or fresh in terms of quality] song which declared the worthiness of the Lamb to open the scroll (with the obvious intent of revealing its message). Christ is qualified to assume this function because of his death (5:9). The death of Jesus, and the victory achieved thereby, is a dominant theme in the Apocalypse (cf. 1:5; 5:12; 7:14; 12:11).

As a consequence of the blood which he shed, the Lamb was able to "purchase" a people for his own possession. Elsewhere this group is identified as the church of the Lord Jesus (Acts 20:28; cf. 1 Cor. 6:19, 20). Notice also that these purchased ones are a "kingdom" – a clear argument that the church and the kingdom constitute the same organism. Moreover, the international nature of the church is emphasized. These citizens of the kingdom are from every nation, and they are serving as priests in the house of God (cf. 1:6; 20:6). John then records: "... and they reign upon the earth" (5:10 – ASV).

First, observe that the "purchased" ones are reigning upon the earth – not the elders, etc., as suggested in the King James Version (contrast "them" with "our"). Second, there is a manuscript variation between "reign" (present tense – ASV) and "shall reign" (future tense – KJV). Which is correct? The context favors the present tense, because the "reigning" is on the part of this kingdom of priests – a circumstance which was present, not future. Jones writes: "Don't make the mistake of deferring this reign to some future millennium. They are reigning now! Remember how Jesus counselled the faithful of Philadelphia to 'hold fast that which thou hast, that no one take thy crown' (3:11)" (p. 31). Leon Morris even concedes: "Some see a reference to a millennarian reign (XX. 4), but this is not necessary" (p. 100).

John then heard a voice, a chorus consisting of thousands upon thousands of beings – angels, the twenty-four elders, and the living creatures. Each was praising the Lamb because of his sacrificial death. As a result of that event, Christ is worthy to receive worship on account of his power, riches, wisdom, might, honor, glory, and blessedness. The seven traits here cataloged perhaps suggest the *complete* adoration that is due the victorious Son of God. In other places in this document, these same qualities are ascribed to the Father (5:13; 7:12) – again, evidence of the divine nature of our Lord.

The final expression of praise (of the five given in chapters 4 and 5) is rendered by "every created thing" that exists – in heaven, on the earth and in the sea, and under the earth (the Hadean realm) – to the glory of both Father and Son. The entire creation acknowledges this truth. Nature's praise of deity is a form of figurative language known as personification (cf. Psa. 148:7-10; Rom. 8:22). Not every human creature worships the Father and Son, of course, but the divine Godhead is *worthy* of such. Finally, to nature's anthem, the four living ones and the elders add their agreement.

What a thrilling duet chapters 4 and 5 of Revelation are. There may not be a more concentrated portion of scripture, detailing the glory of God and his blessed Son, than is found here.

No wonder victory is ours!

CHAPTER 6

SOULS UNDER THE ALTAR OF GOD

Chapter 6 of the book of Revelation begins a series of visions which constitute the prophetic portion of this final section of the New Testament. It has to do with the loosing of the seals of that scroll which the Lamb had taken from the right hand of God. The first four seals, which form a unit, contain the material regarding those images commonly known as "the four horsemen of the Apocalypse." The first horse, a white one, obviously denotes a time of military conquest. The next horse is red. The picture suggested is one of bloodshed. The third animal is a black horse; the accompanying descriptives hint of a time of famine. Finally, the last is a pale horse upon whose back is a rider, denominated as Death and Hades. The picture is one of widespread devastation. The fact that these horsemen are instruments of heavenly judgment is indicated by the multiple usage of "was given" (6:2, 4, 8), which suggests divine permission. Russell Jones says: "The release of these four horsemen unveils to believers the fact that all the great forces of history are definitely related to Christ's permissive will" (p. 34).

To what historical period do these horsemen refer? The answer to that question, of course, depends upon which interpretative viewpoint of the book as a whole one accepts (see "Introduction," Chapter 1). It will be sufficient at this point to say that the vision does not relate to a series of events that are "preparatory to the final consummation" of earthly affairs, as alleged by millennialists (Johnson, p. 472). Many commentators – at least those not of the millennial persuasion – see these visions as prophetic of a time of hardship that the church would experience in the early days of the pagan Roman empire. It is not our purpose in this presentation to speculate as to any specifics connected with the symbols of this context. The focus of this study will be the scene that John was privileged to view relative to the martyred saints who were under the altar of God. For convenience sake, we reproduce the narrative, 6:9-11, as it reads in the ASV.

"And when he opened the fifth seal, I saw underneath the altar the souls of them that had been slain for the word of God, and for the testimony which they held; and they cried with a great voice, saying, How long, O Master, the holy and true, dost thou not judge and avenge our blood on them that dwell on the earth? And there was given them to each one a white robe; and it was said unto them, that they should rest yet for a little time, till their fellow-servants also and their brethren, who should be killed even as they were, should have fulfilled their course."

This divine cup of heavenly revelation effectually runs over with invigorating truth. At the outset, notice that Christ is the one who opens this seal. We must constantly remind ourselves that one of the prevailing themes of this holy treatise is that Jesus is King of kings and Lord of lords. He is in charge of those historical events that are to unfold. No matter how much out-of-hand things appear to be – in terms of human analysis – the Son of God is in control.

In the imagery of the tabernacle motif, John saw the altar of God. Underneath the altar were the souls of those who had been killed on behalf of the cause of Jesus. As the apostle watched, the souls cried out to God, inquiring as to when full justice would be exacted upon their persecutors. It is at this point that we must pause to make two significant remarks.

First, this context establishes the existence of the "soul" as an entity apart of the body. Do human beings possess a "soul"? Many claim that we do not. For example, the "Jehovah's Witnesses" allege that man "does not posses a soul separate and distinct from the body" (**Let God Be True**, p. 349), and, of course, atheists, skeptics, etc., do not concede that the soul exists. However, in the text under consideration, these martyrs were simply "souls" in the presence of God. Their bodies had been buried, burned, thrown to the sea, devoured by wild animals, etc., and yet they existed independently – as *souls*.

The word "soul" is employed in various ways in the Scriptures. It may denote the whole person (1 Pet. 3:20), or merely the life principle that animates a biological body (Gen. 1:30 ASVfn). On the other hand, "soul" may be used of an intelligent, conscious entity that dwells within a human body, or, as in the case under consideration, apart from the body. As the text states, the "souls of *them*" who had been slain. The Bible clearly teaches that human beings possess an essence which is in the "image of God" (Gen. 1:26, 27). This cannot refer to the physical aspect of man, because God is not physical (Jn. 4:24; Lk. 24:39; Mt. 16:17). It must, therefore, denote the soul. Man has *both* a body and soul (Mt. 10:28). We have an "inward" and an "outward" existence, consisting of soul and body (2 Cor. 4:16; cf. Jas. 2:26).

Second, Revelation 6:9ff indicates that the soul is conscious after death. The souls of these martyred saints *spoke* (they cried out to God). They *wondered* ("How long, O Master?"). They *remembered* ("... them that dwell on the earth"). They *reasoned* (concluding that the persecution of God's saints is worthy of punishment) and they *received* (white robes). Too, they *listened* (as they were encouraged to be patient). If these souls were not conscious, language has little meaning.

Elsewhere we have shown, from the narrative concerning the rich man and Lazarus, that there is strong biblical evidence for the consciousness of the dead (Jackson, 1990b, pp. 29, 30). Barnes is quite correct when he observes: "This is one of those incidental proofs in the Bible that the soul does not cease to exist at death, and also that it does not cease to be conscious, or does not sleep till the resurrection" (1954, p. 159).

The souls were underneath the altar of God. They "had been slain." The verb is a perfect tense form, which may suggest the abiding nature of their sacrifice for the Lord. The "altar" is the instrument of offering, and sacrificial blood, during the Levitical period, was poured out at the base of the altar (Lev. 4:7). Perhaps these saints are viewed as having had "fellowship" in the sufferings of the sacrificed Lamb (cf. Phil. 3:10). Why had these ancient children of God been so shamelessly treated? Because of the "word of God, and for the testimony which they held."

Notice that the message they proclaimed was the "word of God" – this is argument for the concept of verbal inspiration. Too, this divine witness, they "held fast" – the verb is in the imperfect tense; they *kept on* holding their testimony, in spite of danger and bloodshed. What faith! Compare this phrase with 1:9; John had been exiled to Patmos for this same reason.

With intense emotion, the martyrs loudly cried out: "How long, O Master, the holy and true [One], dost thou not avenge our blood on them that dwell on the earth?" Reflect upon these thoughts.

(1) Though these disciples had escaped the confines of the earth, and were in the presence of God, they still had questions – hence, were not omniscient. They had not becomes "Gods," as some speculate will be the case.

(2) They designated God as "Master." The Greek word is

despotes, which denotes one who has "absolute ownership and uncontrolled power" (Vine, p. 506). From the human vantage point, it appeared as if the powers of this world held the reins of authority; these glorified martyrs knew better.

(3) The redeemed souls anticipated that justice would be visited upon earth's rebels who abuse the people of God. Why is such an expectation entertained? Because of the *character* of God. He is the "holy and true" One. Some, in their wicked dreams, fancy that God is too benevolent to punish impenitent people. They are wrong. The righteous nature of God will demand that justice be inflicted upon those who have not sought refuge in the Rock of Ages.

(4) Some criticize the attitude of these martyrs, in that they allegedly sought vengeance upon their persecutors. The accusation is misdirected. They were perfectly willing to leave judgment to the Almighty. But the fact is, these saints had been condemned and executed by the court of heathen opinion. They knew their sentence was unjust. They were merely appealing to the Supreme Court for vindication of their cause. Mounce is absolutely correct: "Vindication, not bitter revenge, is the theme" (p. 159). Hendriksen's comment is excellent: "[T]hese martyrs do not invoke retribution for their own sake but for *God's* sake. These saints have been slaughtered because they placed their trust and confidence in God. In slaughtering them, the world has scorned *him!* Does not God himself affirm that the blood of his saints cries for wrath, Gen. 4:10; cf. Heb. 11:4?" (p. 128).

(5) As John observed this sacred scene, he noted that each martyr was given a white robe. The adjective "white" is significantly employed in Revelation (see Chapter 2, "Word Patterns"). It can suggest the idea of purity (7:14), or it may denote the concept of victory (19:11). In this instance, the latter thought

may be more appropriate. As the world viewed it, the saints had been defeated – they were dead and buried. From the divine side, however, the reverse was the case. God, by the gift of this flowing, white robe, acknowledged that these victims had actually won. "Victory" is the keynote theme of this document.

(6) In response to their inquiry, the Lord suggested that they should rest (cf. 14:13) yet for "a little time," until their earth-brethren have fulfilled their course. To what period of history does the "little time" refer? Some feel that it denotes a period of severe persecution in the Roman empire, a condition that was relieved when Constantine finally came to the throne and the persecution of Christians was suspended (Hinds, p. 103). This view, however, overlooks two facts. (a) There were yet centuries of persecution to be endured by God's people (e.g., during the time of the Roman papacy's control of Western civilization). (b) The prayer of the saints appears to be answered in 19:11, when the divine Word comes riding on a white horse from heaven to "judge and make war" on the enemies of his Cause, which is a descriptitive of the Judgment Day. Accordingly, the expression "little time" may be used in a relative sense; time, not as man sees it, but as such is viewed in the divine scheme of things (cf. 2 Pet. 3:8). "The wait of a 'little longer' is in God's estimate but a fleeting moment, though for us it may stretch out for ages (cf. 12:12; 20:3)" (Johnson, p. 475). [Note: This is a point that should not be lost upon those who are addicted to the theory of "realized eschatology." This is the notion that the second coming of Christ must have been realized in the first century, due to the fact that New Testament writers described the Lord's Advent as being near (cf. Jas. 5:8). These folks misunderstand the elastic nature of chronological jargon in *prophetic* literature.]

Revelation 6:9-11 is truly a thrilling vision. Among many

things, it surely teaches that faithful service to the Lord, in spite of the trials and tribulations to which the Christian may be subjected, will be worth it all in the end.

CHAPTER 7

WHO ARE THE ONE HUNDRED FORTY-FOUR THOUSAND?

As we observed earlier, the book of Revelation is a highly symbolic treatise (cf. 1:1). Because of this fact, many false religionists have attempted to exploit the message of the narrative to their own theological ends. The Apocalypse has become a happy hunting ground for some religious cultists who seek biblical support for their peculiar doctrines.

Twice in Revelation, mention is made of a group consisting of 144,000. In chapter 7:1ff, John heard of 144,000 (12,000 each from twelve different Israelite tribes) servants of God who had been sealed on their foreheads. They were thus obviously redeemed people. Also, the apostle saw a "great multitude, which no man can number" out of every nation. These too were redeemed individuals who had been made white in the Lamb's blood. They had victoriously triumphed over tribulation, and served God continuously in his temple. Some feel that these two groups are really the same people – just from different angles.

Again, in Revelation 14:1ff, John saw the Lamb on Mount Zion. With him were 144,000, sealed with the Father's name upon their foreheads. This great multitude had been "purchased out of the earth," and they were said to be the "firstfruits unto God and unto the Lamb."

The "Jehovah's Witnesses" have almost no concept of the distinction between literal and figurative language in the Bible.

And so, they literalize the numeral 144,000 in these two contexts, and ridiculously argue that only 144,000 will ever gain heaven. A Watchtower publication states: "... the final number of the heavenly church will be 144,000, according to God's decree" (**Let God Be True**, p. 113). The balance of humanity, they contend, will live on God's glorified earth (see chapter 13, "A New Heavens and A New Earth").

Chapter 7

There are some minor differences of opinion among reputable Bible scholars as to the identity of the 144,000 in chapter 7. John T. Hinds argued that the number referred to those who were saved from the physical nation of Israel (p. 112).

Others, like J.W. Roberts, felt that this company is spiritual Israel, i.e., the church (p. 71). Some think this group represents the martyrs who have given their lives for the cause of Christ. Be that as it may, it is generally acknowledged that "[t]he number is obviously symbolic. 12 (the number of the tribes) is both squared and multiplied by 1,000 – a twofold way of emphasizing completeness" (Mounce, p. 168).

We must emphasize the following two points: First, one simply cannot take a symbolic section of scripture and interpret it in such a fashion as to make it contradict other clear, literal portions of the Bible.

Second, any doctrine which implies an absurdity is false and must be rejected. The Watchtower theory regarding the 144,000 violates both of these principles. Consider the following observations.

(1) If one argues that the 144,000 represents a literal number, he should similarly contend that the group of which that number consists is also literal, i.e., *literal Israelites*. That would mean, ac-

cording to the Watchtower scheme of interpretation, that no one would be in heaven who was not of the actual tribes listed. This would exclude Abraham, Isaac, and Jacob – who were never of the tribes of Israel. And yet, that conflicts with Jesus' affirmation that Abraham, Isaac, and Jacob will be in the kingdom of *heaven* (Mt. 8:11).

(2) If only a literal 144,000 Israelites will enter heaven, then not one Gentile has the hope of the kingdom of heaven. However, the Lord was plainly alluding to Gentiles when he stated that "many shall come from the east and the west, and shall sit down with Abraham, and Isaac, and Jacob, in the kingdom of heaven" (Mt. 8:11).

(3) If the tribes of chapter 7 are to be literally pressed, not a person from either Ephraim or Dan will enter heaven, for they are excluded from the list. This would mean that such Old Testament heroes as Joshua (from Ephraim) and Samson (from Dan) will not be in heaven. The fact is, mention of the "tribe of Joseph" (7:8), which is not a tribe at all, is evidence of the symbolism of this context.

(4) The Watchtower folk would exclude the "great multitude, which no man could number" (7:9) from heaven. This group, they allege, represents the "earthly class." That is not so. This multitude was said to be "standing before the throne" (7:9), which is in heaven (1:4; 4:2-10). Furthermore, these saints "before the throne" were serving God in "his temple" (7:15). Elsewhere John comments that "the temple of God ... *is in heaven*" (11:19).

Chapter 14

The 144,000 are mentioned again in Revelation 14:1ff. Once more, however, the numeral is clustered among several other prominent symbols. First, there is the "Lamb," a figure representing Christ (cf. Jn. 1:29). Second, there is Mount Zion, a symbol of divine government (cf. Isa. 2:2-4). Third, there is the numeral 144,000, suggestive of the completeness of God's people – no one will be missing who is supposed to be there. Fourth, the saints are described as "virgins," which descriptive emphasizes their purity (cf. 2 Cor. 11:2). Again, though, it must be stressed that if one contends for a literal 144,000, he should also, if he would be consistent, argue that a literal Lamb was literally standing on literal Mount Zion with a group of literal men who were literally virgins!

If a consistent literal scheme of interpretation were thus pursued, here is the situation that would obtain:

(1) Only *men* will be in heaven, hence, Mary, Dorcus, Hannah, and women of like faith are without that hope.

(2) Only *unmarried* men, virgins, will gain heaven. This would exclude Abraham, Moses, Peter, and a host of other biblical worthies.

These conclusions, though consistent with the line of argumentation reviewed above, are utterly ludicrous and without any merit whatever.

The 144,000 of chapter 14 likely signifies the entire body of the redeemed. They were "purchased" from among men. The only purchase price ultimately available for human salvation is that of the blood of Jesus Christ. His blood was effective for the obedient who lived before the cross (Gal. 4:5; Heb. 9:15-17), and for those who have lived since that historic event (1 Pet. 1:18, 19; Acts 20:28).

Finally, as we shall demonstrate in a later chapter, *no one* will live eternally on earth (see Chapter 13, "A New Heavens and A New Earth").

CHAPTER 8

THE MARK OF THE BEAST (PART 1)

Revelation 13:11ff describes a horrible beast that ascends from the earth. Many people are described as receiving a strange "mark" – the beast's mark. Reception of this mark carries dreadful consequences.

There may not be a more frightening thought, in reflecting upon the book of Revelation, than that of the possibility of receiving the "mark of the beast." And such a dread is not without justification. The "mark" associated with "the beast" is mentioned seven times in the Apocalypse (13:16, 17; 14:9, 11; 16:2; 19:20; 20:4). In some manuscripts the term is also found in 15:2.

As this study is begun, it will be very helpful, in identifying the "mark of the beast," if we can summarize the divine information that is given regarding this figure. First, though, we must remind ourselves again that we are dealing with symbols. One is not to look for some literal "mark" or "brand" that is to be cut or burned into the actual flesh of certain people. The "mark" represents an idea. Consider the following characteristics.

Traits of the Mark of the Beast

(1) The mark is received upon the "right hand" or upon the "forehead" (13:16; 14:9; 20:4). The allusion to the "right hand" may signify that the one receiving the mark was extending "the right hand of fellowship" (Gal. 2:9) to certain error. This would indicate that the marked person had participated in the beast's teaching and practices. Receiving the beast's mark upon the fore-

head may suggest receiving a sign of *identification* – in much the same way that the Lord's servants have the names of God and Christ "written on their foreheads" (14:1; cf. 3:12). Too, the language may suggest an *intellectual reception* of dogma. The combined ideas may thus reflect the concept of believing and practicing doctrines that are antagonistic to the will of Jehovah God.

(2) The influence of the beast is extensive. He causes "all [a synecdoche for "many"], the small and the great, the rich and the poor, and the free and the bond" to receive his mark (13:16). Vast multitudes will fall under his diabolical control.

(3) Those who do not receive the mark of the beast will be persecuted. An economic symbol is employed to convey this idea. The unmarked person will not be allowed to buy or to sell (13:17). Compare similar symbolism in 6:5, 6.

(4) The number signifies the "name" of a "man" (13:17, 18; 14:11; 15:2). It is very important to keep this point in view.

(5) In order to decode the mystery of the man's name (which will require "wisdom"), the number representing his name must be "counted" (13:18). Note the use of the term *psephizo* in Luke 14:28 (the only other occurrence in the New Testament) where it denotes calculating, i.e., adding up, the cost of a thing. Mounce says that this descriptive "is an invitation to work backwards from the number 666 to the name for which it is the numerical equivalent" (pp. 263, 264). Each letter in the Greek alphabet represents a numerical value. *Alpha*=1, *beta*=2, *iota*=10, etc. Deissmann quotes an inscription from ancient Pompey in which a man says: "I love her whose number is 545" (quoted by Mounce, p. 263). The letters in his sweetheart's name totalled 545. One must look for a similar situation in interpreting the 666. Zahn notes that John's "readers could and had to understand him in

no other way, than that the numerical values of the letters of the personal name written in Greek are *summed up* in the number 666" (p. 445; emp. WJ).

(6) Those who receive the mark of the beast are involved in false religion; they "worship" the beast (13:15; 14:9, 11; 16:2; 19:20; 20:4). The beast is not a mere abstraction.

(7) There are those who refuse to yield to the beast and his mark; they are "victorious" over him (15:2). They "reign" with Christ (20:4).

(8) Those who received the mark of the beast were recipients of divinely permitted plagues (16:2), and ultimately they will be punished eternally (14:9-11; 19:20, 21).

Any theory regarding the "mark of the beast" that does not take into consideration these traits, is one that does not meet the biblical criteria.

The Mark of the Beast: Popular Theories

Before we set forth the case for what we believe is the most reasonable view of "the mark of the beast," we wish to consider some of the popular ideas that are associated with this theme. We will not give any credence to those bizarre notions which connect the mark of the beast with the Social Security system, credit cards, or patent medicine, etc.! We will not even consider the Adventist notion that worshiping on Sunday is the mark of the beast (Damsteegt, p. 167).

(1) Dispensationalists contend that the beast, described in Revelation 13:11-18, is a sinister character who will appear shortly before the second coming of Christ. They call him "the *Antichrist*." (see Scofield, Note on Rev. 13:16).

There are two major problems with this idea. First, dispensationalism, as a theological scheme, is false from beginning to end.

Its view of the "mark of the beast" is thus equally erroneous (see chapter 11, "The Battle of Armageddon").

Second, the Bible simply does not describe a solitary sinister person, to appear in the final days of the Christian age, who is designated as "the Antichrist."

The term "antichrist" is found five times in four New Testament passages (1 Jn. 2:18 (twice); 2:22; 4:3; 2 Jn. 7). Consider these facts. (a) The apostle John is the only New Testament writer to employ the word, and *he never uses it in Revelation* – which is supposed to be dominated by the presence of the Antichrist! Strange indeed. (b) As suggested above, the expression "antichrist" is not applied to an exclusive individual; rather, there are many "antichrists" (1 Jn. 2:18). (c) Antichrist is not some evil person who first arises in the 20th century, for "antichrists" were operative in the days of the apostle John (1 Jn. 2:18; 2:22; 4:3; 2 Jn. 7). Especially notice the verbal tenses in these passages. Nothing regarding "antichrist" in the Bible conforms to the dispensational theory. For further discussion of the tenants of dispensationalism, see chapter 12, "The Thousand-Year Reign of Christ."

(2) Some identify the beast of Revelation 13:11ff, and the reception of his mark, as devotion to the "Caesar cult" in the early centuries of the church's history, though perhaps not confined to that antique culture. Jones thinks "[t]his beast represents for all time the whole anti-Christian effort to turn men from the true God to false divinities, under the sponsorship of some pagan government. This beast may at one time be the Caesar cult of Rome, at another the gestapo of Hitler, at another the secret spies of the Kremlin, at another the agents of Red China ..." (p. 71).

According to this view, whereas "seven" is the common number in Revelation for perfection, "six" must stand for imperfection. And so, 666 becomes the "trinity of imperfection" (cf. Mounce,

p. 265). Hendriksen adopts this notion and calls 666 "failure upon failure upon failure" (p. 182; cf. Jones, p. 70; Smith, 1963, p. 1513). A major problem with this view of 666 is the fact that it does not correspond to the specific description of the number (e.g., requiring "counting" the number, etc.) as that information is set forth in Revelation 13:18 (read again point number five, p. 60).

(3) Possibly the most popular view held today regarding the mark of the beast is the concept that 666 is an allusion to the Roman ruler, Nero. Several denominationalists have argued this viewpoint (cf. Barclay, 1959, p. 133), and so have some within churches of Christ (Roberts, pp. 115, 116; Bright, p. 448).

We believe this viewpoint to be faulty on several grounds. (a) The book of Revelation, composed c. A.D. 96, is a book of *prophecy* dealing with events *to come*. Nero died in A.D. 68. It seems unlikely, therefore, that he would be the focus of Revelation 13. (b) Those who allege that the letters "Caesar Nero" add up to 666 must resort to some strange manipulation to achieve the coveted result, e.g., changing the name from Greek to Hebrew, adding the title "Caesar" to the emperor's name, and then deleting one letter from the appellation. That is truly an example of manipulating the text. (c) Irenaeus, who lived around A.D. 130-200, discussed several possible solutions to deciphering 666, yet he never included Nero in the list (**Against Heresies**, V.30). (d) The designation "Nero Caesar," as a solution to 666, was not even suggested as a possibility until 1831 (Zahn, p. 447). The case for "Nero Caesar," as the meaning of 666, is seriously lacking in support.

What, then, does the number 666 signify? Before we are prepared to consider that, some background study must be pursued. That will be the thrust of the following chapter.

CHAPTER 9

THE MARK OF THE BEAST (PART 2)

There is one point upon which virtually all conservative Bible scholars are agreed. It is this: there is an obvious connection between Daniel, chapter 7, and the 13th chapter of the book of Revelation. Leon Morris notes that the first beast of Revelation 13 "combines in himself the horrors" that are "distributed among the four" beasts of Daniel 7 (p. 165; cf. Barclay, 1959, p. 109; Hendriksen, p. 177; Mounce, p. 249). Burton Coffman is absolutely correct when he says that Daniel 7 is "the key to the interpretation" of Revelation 13 (1979, p. 293).

Daniel saw four beasts come up from the sea (7:3). The first was like a lion, the second was a bear, the third a leopard, and the fourth was diverse from the others; it had ten horns (7:4-8). John observed two beasts. One came from the sea, the other from the earth. The first was like a lion, bear, and leopard; and yet, it was diverse, with seven heads and ten horns (13:1, 2). In Daniel's dream a "little horn" came out of the fourth beast. It had eyes, a mouth, and it spoke great things (7:8). In Revelation 13, the beast that came up from the earth was like a lamb, but it spoke as a dragon (13:11). According to Daniel, the "little horn" made war with the saints and prevailed against them (7:21), whereas in John's vision, the sea-beast also made war with the saints and overcame them (13:7). Daniel's "little horn" spoke words against the most high (7:25); John's initial beast spoke blasphemies against God (13:6). Finally, according to Daniel, the saints were "given into his [the little horn's] hand" for a time, times, and a half a time (7:25) – which is equivalent to forty-two months, or 1,260 days (cf. Rev. 11:2, 3; 12:6, 14). In Revelation 13, the sea beast was granted authority to continue his diabolical work for forty-two months (13:5). The following lists should help to demonstrate the concurrence between Daniel 7 and Revelation 13.

Daniel 7

- Lion (4)
- Bear (5)
- Leopard (6)
- Ten Horns (7)
- Little Horn (8)
- Spake Great Things (8)
- War With Saints (21)
- Prevail Against Them (21)
- Speak Words Against Most High (25)
- For Time, Times, Half A Time (25)

Revelation 13

- Lion (2)
- Bear (2)
- Leopard (2)
- Ten Horns (1)
- Like Lamb (11)
- Spake Like Dragon (11)
- War With Saints (7)
- Overcome Them (7)
- Speak Blasphemies Against God (6)
- Continue Forty-Two Months (5)

The careful student will have noticed that the ten characteristics listed are a composite of all the beasts in Daniel 7, and both beasts in Revelation 13. And this is not surprising at all. The close relationships and common interests of these beasts "would naturally lead them to manifest the same traits" (Hinds, p. 192). It is not unusual, therefore, that what is said regarding one, is often spoken concerning another. Sometimes the connection is so intimate that it is scarcely possible to distinguish one from the other (cf. 13:12).

In view of the clear connection between Daniel 7 and Revelation 13, surely a careful study of Daniel's vision can be of great service in unlocking the significance of Revelation 13, including the enigmatic "mark of the beast."

The Prophecy of Daniel's "Little Horn"

In the second year of Nebuchadnezzar's reign over the Babylonian empire (ca. 603 B.C.), Daniel, a Hebrew in captivity, was called upon to reveal and interpret a dream for the monarch. He told of a great image in the form of a man consisting of four sections. The head was of gold, its breast and arms were silver, the belly and thighs were fashioned of brass, and the legs were iron – the feet being iron mingled with clay. The image was struck on its feet by a stone that had been cut (without human hands) from a mountain. The metallic image was destroyed and the stone itself became a mountain filling the entire earth (Dan. 2:31-35).

The meaning of the dream was clear. The golden head represented the Neo-Babylonian empire (626-539 B.C.). That government would be followed by the kingdom of the Medes and Persians (539-332 B.C.). The Medo-Persian empire would be succeeded by the Greek regime (332-63 B.C.), which in turn would finally give way to Roman rule (63 B.C. - A.D. 476). During the era of the Roman empire, God himself would set up his kingdom, which would be a universal, spiritual monarchy

(Dan. 2:44). The divinely initiated dream occurred almost seventy years before the Babylonian empire fell and is a remarkable example of prophecy. The dramatic revelations in this book of future international events, provide the basis for the liberal motive which seeks to discredit Daniel as the author of the narrative, ascribing it to some unknown person of the 2nd century B.C.

About a half century later, in the first year of Belshazzar (a grandson of Nebuchadnezzar), Daniel himself had a dream and visions which, to a significant degree, had a thrust similar to the prophetic dream entertained by Nebuchadnezzar. From the turbulent "great sea" he saw four diverse beasts successively rise. Without question, these four beasts correspond to the four metallic components of the image portrayed in chapter 2.

The Lion

The first beast was like a lion, but it also had eagle's wings. As Daniel watched, the wings were torn off. The lion stood up like a man and a human heart was given to it. This initial beast represented the Babylonian empire. Concerning Nebuchadnezzar, Jeremiah wrote: "A lion is gone up from his thicket, and a destroyer of nations; he is on his way, he is gone forth from his place, to make your land desolate, that your cities be laid waste, without inhabitant" (Jer. 4:7). He further declared: "Our pursuers were swifter than the eagles of the heavens" (Lam. 4:19). The rapid campaigns against Assyria, Egypt, and Palestine are graphically depicted in the symbolism. But the advancement of the Babylonian conquest was stayed (the wings plucked). Moreover, it is a matter of historical record that during the latter era of the Babylonian regime there was a "gradual diminution of the ferocity of conquest under a succession of comparatively weak princes" (Barnes, 1853, p. 290).

The Bear

The second beast was like a bear, an animal noted for its fierceness (cf. Hos. 13:8). This bear was higher on one side than on the other. Since the beast represents the Medo-Persian kingdom (as indicated by the silver portion of the earlier image), this would suggest that one of these national powers would overshadow the other (cf. 8:3, 20). This conforms to the actual facts. In their early history, the Persians were subject to the Medes, but Cyrus conquered the king of Media in 558 B.C., and supremacy passed to the Persians. The bear had three ribs in its mouth, likely reflecting the fact that this empire had conquered the nations of Lydia (546 B.C.), Babylon (539 B.C.), and Egypt (525 B.C.). This vision occurs when Babylon was at the zenith of her power and in no apparent danger of falling.

The Leopard

The third creature was like a leopard with wings upon its back. It also had four heads. The winged leopard, of course, hints of blazing speed. This signifies the conquests of the Greek regime under Alexander the Great. See Daniel 8:5 and 21 where the "king of Greece" moves so rapidly that his feet "touched not the ground."

Alexander came to the Macedonian throne when he was but twenty years of age; by the time he was twenty-five he was virtual master of the Eastern world. At the battle of Arbela, with a force of less than 50,000 men, he defeated Darius whose army was 600,000 strong. It is also significant that the leopard of Daniel's vision had four heads. Remarkably, this signifies the fate of his empire following his death. Alexander had no heir, consequently his territories were divided among four of his generals. Lysimachus took nearly the whole of Asia Minor; Cassander had Greece;

Seleucus possessed Syria and the East; while Ptolemy claimed Egypt and Palestine (Sanderson, et. al., p. 132). This is further confirmed by the testimony of chapter 8, verses 8, 22. Remember, Daniel is seeing a vision of events that were not to transpire for more than 200 years!

The Ten-Horned Beast

Finally, the prophet saw a fourth beast emerge from the sea. It was different from the preceding animals. It was terrible, with great iron teeth and nails of brass. This beast crushed its enemies and stamped the residue with its feet. Moreover, this animal had ten horns. This fourth beast (or kingdom – vs. 23), corresponds to the fourth segment of the earlier image (iron and iron-clay – ch. 2); it is the Roman empire.

Interestingly, as these empires come and go, there is a *degeneration* suggested (i.e., from gold to iron, etc.). It is clear that Daniel "was not encouraged to see in history evolutionary progress, but rather the reverse. Modern technological progress in no way invalidates this judgment, for it is international justice, peace and human contentment and fulfillment that are in mind, and in these realms it would be hard to argue that there has been progress" (Baldwin, p. 140).

Some contend that the beast's "ten horns" are but a figurative representation of the political descendants of the old Roman empire and thus the numeral is not to be pressed (Young, p. 149). Others assert that when Rome fell in A.D. 476, the result was the formation of ten literal states or governments. Newton, citing Whitson, says that "the number of the kingdoms into which the Roman empire in Europe ... was originally divided ... was exactly ten" (Newton, p. 234).

As the prophet was meditating upon the significance of the

ten horns, he saw a "little horn" uproot three of the other horns. This little horn had eyes like a man and a mouth that spoke great things, hinting of a personal force rather than mere political abstraction.

Several other characteristics of the little horn are subsequently mentioned: (a) The little horn represented a force that was "more stout" than the other governments; (b) it "made war with the saints" and attempted to "wear out" the people of God; (c) it prevailed against the saints until the Lord gave a judgment on behalf of his people; (d) the little horn would "speak words against the Most High"; (e) it [he] would "think to change the times and the law" of God; (f) the saints were given into his hand for "a time, times, and half a time." Exactly who (or what) was this infamous "little horn"?

The Little Horn

Let us carefully consider some suggestions that have been made regarding the identity of the little horn in Daniel's vision.

(1) Religious modernism contends that the little horn was Antiochus Epiphanes (ruled 175-164 B.C.), the Syrian rogue who so viciously persecuted the Jews during the interbiblical era (cf. Dan. 8:9-14; 23-27). As we mentioned earlier, due to the fact that the prophetical sections of Daniel are so very precise, modernists, rejecting the concept of predictive prophecy, allege that the book of Daniel was the composition of some unknown scribe of the second century B.C. Thus, according to this theory, the document addresses the past, not the future. The persecuting little horn is conveniently identified with Antiochus. This position was apparently first set forth by Porphyry, a philosopher (A.D. 3rd Cent.), who sought to discredit the Bible as inspired revelation.

This theory simply will not work. The fact is, Antiochus lived in the period of Greek supremacy. He was dead a hundred years before the fourth beast (the Roman empire) came into power – out of which the little horn arose. That aside, there is clear and convincing evidence that the book of Daniel was written in the sixth century B.C., not in the 2nd century (see Jackson, 1990c pp. 30, 31). [Note: The "little horn" of Daniel 8:9ff is a reference to Antiochus, but this must not be confused with the "little horn" of chapter 7.]

Attempts have been made to identify the beasts of Daniel's dream in the following fashion – Babylonians, Medes, Persians, Greeks – so as to allow the little horn to appear in the fourth (Greek) period. It is not, however, a legitimate procedure to separate the Medo-Persian empire into two segments. There was no Median empire, separate from the Persian regime, which could be called a world power (Rose & Fuller, p. 336).

(2) Modern millennialists assert that the little horn of Daniel's dream is the "Antichrist" who soon will make his presence known to initiate a persecution against the church. Allegedly, this will introduce the Tribulation Period which is supposed to precede the return of Christ and his 1,000-year reign from Jerusalem (see Pentecost, p. 1355). There are insurmountable obstacles to this view. In the first place, the entire premillennial scheme, including the Antichrist and Tribulation components, is without biblical support. No interpretation of Daniel 7 is legitimate which depends upon a theological theory that is so at variance with fundamental Bible truth – which the premillennial theory clearly is (see the author's booklet, **Premillennialism – A System of Infidelity**).

Second, the little horn of Daniel's vision arose from the remnants of the Roman empire, which have lain in the dust of antiquity for more than 1,500 years. The commencement of the little horn's power is thus ancient, not modern. Sensing the difficulty in this fact, millennialists allege that the old Roman empire will be *revived* in these modern times to accommodate Bible prophecy! There is absolutely no support for this incredible speculation. [Note: Some, who are not of the premillennial persuasion, also believe that the little horn is a sinister Antichrist personality who will appear shortly before the Lord's return. For reasons which will be apparent subsequently, we reject this view as well.]

(3) Some argue that the little horn represents one of the pagan Roman rulers, e.g., Julius Caesar or Vespasian. However, as a great variety of biblical scholars have forcefully argued, Daniel's "little horn" and Paul's "man of sin" (2 Thes. 2:3ff) appear to represent the *same* hostile force. This was the general view of the "church fathers" (see Newton, pp. 462, 463), and such has been maintained in modern times. Since the "man of sin" is obviously a part of "the falling away" from the primitive faith, the opposing force would seem to be an *apostate religious* one, and that would eliminate a Caesar (see Appendix II, "Who is Paul's 'Man of Sin'?", cf. also Workman, pp. 414-436).

(4) An interpretation which has fallen on hard times in this modern ecumenical age, but which was strongly defended by scholars of the reformation heritage (e.g., Elliott, Newton, Clarke, Barnes, etc.), is the concept that Daniel's little horn symbolized the *papal dynasty*. A few conservative scholars defend this position even yet (Leupold, p. 323). Too, this was the leading view of the restoration leaders. When Alexander Campbell met John Purcell in debate (1837), he affirmed that the Roman Catholic Church "is the Babylon of John, the Man of Sin of Paul, and the Empire of the Youngest Horn of Daniel's Sea Monster" (pp. 281ff). Consider the following arguments which lend sup-

port to this proposition.

(a) Prior to the 8th century A.D., the authority of the Catholic popes was limited to church affairs. However, near the middle of that century the Roman pontiff began to acquire political territories, thus transforming the Church into a politico-ecclesiastical organism. In A.D. 755, Pepin, a French ruler, conferred upon pope Stephen III the principality of Ravenna. Later, in 774, Charles the Great, monarch of France, conquered the kingdom of the Lombards and gave their dominion to pope Adrian I. Finally, in 817, Lewis the Pious, son of Charles the Great, confirmed the state of Rome to pope Paschal I. The Roman church was the most powerful force in Europe – a little horn that became more stout than its fellows. By the time cardinal Hildebrand became pope (1073), he was affirming that the Roman pontiff should not only be the universal head of the church, but also the ruler of the world (cf. Newton, pp. 241-245; Sanderson, pp. 334-336).

(b) The little horn was said to speak "great things" which were "against the Most High." The blasphemous arrogance of the popes is well-known to students of church history. Newton cites the following papal claim: "Our Lord God the pope; another God upon earth, king of kings, and lord of lords. The same is the dominion of God and the pope. To believe that our Lord God the pope might not decree, as he decreed, it were a matter of heresy. The power of the pope is greater than all created power, and extends itself to things celestial, terrestrial, and infernal. The pope doeth whatsoever he listeth, even things unlawful, and is more than God" (p. 456). Pope Innocent III (1198-1216), in his inaugural speech, declared: "The successor of St. Peter stands midway between God and man; below God, above man; Judge of all, judged of none" (Hurlbut, 1954a, p. 112).

(c) The Roman church, under the authority of its popes, has

been a vicious persecutor of those who oppose its apostate doctrines. A Catholic scholar asserts that his church "... can tolerate no strange Churches beside herself ..." (Pohle, p. 766). During the Spanish Inquisition (a tribunal established by the Catholic Church in the Middle Ages for the purpose of suppressing error) thousands were burned alive for their alleged heresies against the Church. During the infamous massacre of St. Bartholomew's day (August 24, 1572) somewhere between 20,000 and 100,000 Protestants were killed near Paris. A Catholic historian admits: "On 8 September a procession of thanksgiving took place in Rome, and the pope, in a prayer after mass, thanked God for having 'granted the Catholic people a glorious triumph over a perfidious race'" (Goyau, p. 337).

(d) The little horn would alter the "times and the law" of God. According to Catholic dogma, ecclesiastical authority and tradition carry as much weight, if not more, than the Word of God itself (see Attwater, p. 41). Thus, the Church feels free to change or make religious laws as it sees fit. History is replete with examples of the papacy instituting holy seasons and days, and changing various elements of the law of Christ (e.g., celibacy, adoration of images, saint worship, transubstantiation, etc.).

(e) The saints were to be under the oppressive power of the little horn for "a time, times, and half a time." Clearly, this is the most difficult aspect of the prophecy. A number of novel views have been suggested as to the significance of this expression. The most reasonable conclusion is that it likely represents three and one half year's worth of prophetic days, i.e., a total of 1,260 days, symbolizing 1,260 years (as in the case of the seventy weeks of chapter 9) (cf. Rev. 12:6, 14; 13:5). The knotty part is knowing what period of history this time span actually covers. It would seem to point to that era when Roman Catholicism almost completely dominated and suppressed the religious world, until its power was broken by the influence of the reformation movement. It is not necessary to look for precise dates for the beginning and ending of the period.

In conclusion, we believe that, taking all factors into consideration, there is no entity in history that so precisely fits the description of the "little horn" of Daniel 7, as that of the papal dynasty of the Roman Catholic Church.

CHAPTER 10

THE MARK OF THE BEAST (PART 3)

If our view of Daniel 7 is correct, the complementary elements between Daniel 7 and Revelation 13 would seem to suggest that the latter is describing the aggressive and hostile nature of the Roman empire, and the papal system which grew out of it. These companion institutions vigorously sought to oppose the righteous cause of true Christianity. Clearly, as Mounce states, we are here "introduced to the two agents through whom Satan carries out his war against believers" (p. 248).

We will not discuss the intricate details of Revelation 13:1-17, since most of these have been dealt with in the previous chapter of this book in connection with Daniel 7. However, a few observations are in order.

The Sea Beast

The first beast that John observes rises from the sea. Note that Satan is standing "by the sand of the sea" (13:1), suggesting that the beast derives its power from this arch-enemy of God. We believe this first beast represents the old, pagan Roman empire, which corresponds to the fourth beast of Daniel 7.

Many commentators agree. Mounce says there is "little doubt" that this beast is the Roman empire (p. 251). Roberts contends: "It seems clear that the first beast represents Imperial Rome ..." (p. 108). Clarke comments: "The beast here described is the Latin empire ..." (p. 1016). G.R. Beasley-Murray agrees (p. 1295). Newton declared that most writers – ancient and modern, Catholic and protestant – believe this beast to "represent the Roman empire" (p. 605; cf. Barnes, 1954, p. 321).

The monster had seven heads and ten horns. For the significance of the ten horns, see Chapter 9 (p. 70). The seven heads apparently signify seven kinds of government (cf. 17:9, 10, where the seven heads of the beast are seven mountains, or seven kings – a symbol for government – cf. Isa. 2:2-4; 11:9; Dan. 2:35; 7:17, 23). This imagery would suggest that the Roman empire had been characterized by various and successive forms of government.

John notes that one of the beast's seven heads had received a death-like wound; but, amazingly, the wound was healed. It is a matter of historical record that the pagan Roman empire, in the mid-fifth century A.D., was invaded by a number of barbarian tribes from the north. Hurlbut states: "By these successive invasions and disruptions, the once vast empire of Rome was reduced to a little territory around the capital" (1954a, p. 97). The Roman empire had been given a death-blow indeed.

It is believed by many that Rome's death-stroke was "healed" by the growing amalgamation between the empire and the corrupt church of that day. Henry Alford identified the "healing" with "the establishment of the Christian [papal] Roman Empire" (p. 1884). Barnes said that "the monster had received a fatal wound, until its power was restored by the influence of the spiritual domination of the church of Rome." He says that pagan Rome "would have wholly and for ever ceased if it had not been restored – the deadly wound being healed – by the influence of the Papal power ..." (1954, p. 322). One cannot but recall the *intimate connection* between the fourth beast of Daniel's vision (chapter 7), and the little horn that plucked up three of the beast's horns (see Chapter 9, p. 67). One writer expresses it in this fashion. By the union of church and state, "political Rome revived as a persecuting power ... it became the agent through which papal Rome (the apostate church) continued the persecutions" (Hinds, p. 191).

As one considers the balance of the information regarding the sea-beast (13:1-10), this important point must be kept in view. From the time the deadly head-wound was received (by imperial Rome), and then was healed, the description is no longer of a strictly heathen power. Rather, the focus of the narrative is now on a *politico-ecclesiastical* organism, the pagan-papal combination. Keep this in mind when you read that this beast blasphemes, makes war with the saints, and overcomes them for forty-two months (i.e., 1,260 years), etc. For a discussion of these details, see Chapter 9, where such matters are discussed in connection with the hurtful influence of Daniel's "little horn."

The corrupt state-church organism exerted tremendous influence in the antique world (13:7). As Clarke observed, the reference is to the "Latin world" (p. 1019), and not to the globe as a whole (cf. Lk. 2:1). Thousands upon thousands worshiped (i.e., submitted to) the beast.

There were exceptions, of course. Those whose names were written in the Lamb's book of life (13:8), did not yield to the domination of the sea-monster. The ones who were enrolled in the book of life were Christians. The conditions of Heaven's redemptive plan (the death of Christ and gospel obedience) were determined from the "foundation of the world," hence it might be said that the saints' names were written at that time. This is the concept reflected in the ASV. The KJV leaves the impression that it was the death of Christ that was determined from the beginning of time. In any case, there is no justification in this passage for the Calvinistic dogma of predestination.

The Earth Beast

The second half of Revelation 13 begins with verse 11 and continues through the balance of the chapter. John saw "another" beast arise. The word "another" is important. It translates the Greek term *allos*, which suggests another of the same kind. What or who is the second beast? We do not believe that the identification is to be found in "the priesthood of the cult of the emperor" (Beasley-Murray, p. 1296), or the "Antichrist" who arises at the close of the age (Scofield, Note on Rev. 13:16; Smith, 1963, p. 1513).

Even those who do not subscribe to the "historical" approach to Revelation agree that the second beast of Revelation 13 is a decidedly *religious* movement. Jones comments that the use of "lamb" as a descriptive of the beast "indicates that this power was connected with religion," since "lamb" hints of sacrifice to deity (p. 68). William Lee stated that whereas the "first Beast is a material, political, World-power; the second Beast is a spiritual World-power" (p. 671). Elsewhere this beast appears to be synonymous with the "false prophet" (cf. 16:13; 19:20; 20:10).

Henry Alford says that the second beast is the "reviver and the upholder of the first [beast]" (see 13:3, 12). He asserts that the beast is "Latin Christianity, in its ecclesiastico-secular form" (p. 1886). Alford thought this movement includes the Roman papacy, but that Romanism does not exhaust the meaning of the symbol. Adam Clarke believed the second beast to be "the spiritual Latin empire, or, in other words, the Romish hierarchy; for with no other power can the prophetic description ... be shown to accord" (p. 1020). Coffman called it "a perverted religion of Christ" (1979, p. 303).

Other scholars have argued the same position. Albert Barnes, with great force, pled this case, as did our own John T. Hinds

(Gospel Advocate commentary). Earlier we mentioned Alexander Campbell's affirmation of this proposition in his famous debate with Catholic Bishop John Purcell. Too, B.W. Johnson, a brother of the American restoration heritage, wrote a book titled, **A Vision of the Ages**, which identifies the second beast with the papal dynasty. More recently, the highly esteemed Hugo McCord has argued that the second beast of Revelation is papal Rome (pp. 399-405). We must say, with all candor, that we believe this view has not been given a fair hearing by most of our modern brethren.

Thomas Newton's (1704-1782) famous work, **Dissertations on the Prophecies**, which Bickersteth characterized as "a very valuable work," is filled with documentation which supports this view. Also, we must not neglect to mention E.B. Elliott, who authored a massive, four-volume set titled, **Horae Apocalypticae**. Elliott contended that the second beast is the "Papal Clergy" (p. 162). Spurgeon called Elliott's treatment of the Apocalypse "the standard work on the subject." Consider the traits of this land-beast.

(a) It has two horns. Horns symbolize power, perhaps suggestive of a dual, church-state authority.

(b) It appears like a lamb (a *Christian* symbol, suggesting meekness, one offering atonement, etc.), but speaks like a dragon. Every student of church history is familiar with the arrogant dictums of the papacy, which claims to be head of the church and ruler of the world – though, of necessity, this force is somewhat muted in modern times due to the Bible's influence.

(c) It exercised the authority of the first beast, the state, thus was both religious and civil.

(d) It feigned "great signs" (similar to what Elijah did in the Old Testament in calling down fire from heaven). We have employed the word "feigned" because God does not authenticate false religion with genuine miracles. Nor can Satan work true miracles. If he could, his dogma would have credentials comparable to the Lord's. Rather, these are "lying wonders" (cf. 2 Thes. 2:9). The miraculous claims of Catholicism, of course, are legion (see Appendix II).

(e) The beast was a persecuting force, killing many.

(f) It is specifically identified as having a designation that is the letter-numeral equivalent of 666.

Burton Coffman describes the second beast as the apostasy which occurred in the "historical church." And, in his characteristically blunt fashion, he asks: "What is to be thought of the 'Christian scholars' who are either ignorant of this, or who do not have the guts to mention it?" (1979, pp. 291, 292).

The Mysterious 666

Now, at long last, we are ready to consider the meaning of the cryptic 666. We believe that the best evidence indicates that 666 represents the ancient name, *Lateinos*, a Latin king, who was reputed to be the founder of the Latin empire (Campbell, p. 287; Schaff, 1980, p. 844). Consider the following factors:

(1) The name *Lateinos*, in Greek, is rendered as follows: L(30) A(1) T(300) E(5) I(10) N(50) O(70) S(200), which equals 666. This is not conclusive of itself, but it is a starting place.

(2) The identification with *Lateinos* goes back to the very shadow of the apostolic age. Phillip Schaff concedes that it is "the oldest [view] we know of" (1980, p. 844). Irenaeus (c. A.D. 130-200), a disciple of Polycarp, who was reputedly converted by the apostle John, mentions *Lateinos* as a "very probable" possibility for the meaning of the 666 (though he actually prefers another designation). Similarly, Hippolytus (c. A.D. 170-236), a disciple

of Irenaeus, suggested that 666 may point to *Lateinos*. Elliott also says that "*Andreas*, another learned Greek Father who lived some three centuries later, retained the word *Lateinos*, as one of the admissible solutions" (p. 211).

(3) We must emphasize, however, that it requires more than mere letter/numeral equivalency to identify the 666. As Newton pointed out, along "with the name also the other qualities and properties of the beast must all agree. The name alone will not constitute agreement; all other particulars must be perfectly applicable ..." (p. 619). This factor clearly eliminates names like Mussolini, Hitler, and Martin Luther – which some have argued make as much sense as the designation, *Lateinos*.

The fact of the matter is, it would be hard to find a designation more fitting to symbolize the papal system than that of *Lateinos*, meaning "the Latin man." If the Catholic Church has been anything, she has been a Latin Church. Newton, citing Dr. Henry Moore, observes that the Roman Church Latinizes virtually everything within its grasp – masses, prayers, hymns, litanies, canons, decretals, bulls, etc. The Council of Trent decreed that the Latin Vulgate is the only authentic version (p. 619).

When all has been said, we believe that the case which contends that the second beast of Revelation is corrupt, persecuting papal Rome, is a very strong one.

But two objections are commonly made to this position. First, it is alleged that this view would have little relevance to the original recipients of the book. In response we must note:

(a) This objection could be made of any segment of the book that points beyond the first century. Shall we contend (as those advocating realized eschatology do) that the entire book of Revelation was fulfilled within the first century? Surely that is an extreme position.

(b) What relevance does *any* prophecy, which extends hundreds of years into the future, have to the people contemporary with the original utterance? Shall we argue that the book of Daniel does not prophesy concerning the kingdom of Christ (2:44) because the Hebrews in Babylonian Captivity would never see the oracle fulfilled? One is not thinking clearly when he argues in this fashion.

Second, it is claimed that since there is such a wide interpretative range regarding the beasts, and the meaning of 666, surely this cannot be the correct view. Such logic would negate *any* view of Revelation 13, or the entire book for that matter. If objections are to be raised against the concept that 666 reflects the rise of that politico-ecclesiastical system which dominated Christian history for more than a thousand years, then let it be done with substantial arguments – not superficial quibbles.

As we conclude this chapter, we cannot but raise this engaging question. Does it seem likely that a book, dealing with the enemies of God's church, would overlook one of the most formidable foes that the body of Christ has ever had? Paul certainly spoke of a movement that represented a "falling away" from the faith (2 Thes. 2:1ff; see Appendix II). Did John completely ignore the same movement? Coffman is right on target when he writes: "[T]here are at least seven whole chapters of the New Testament devoted to that phenomenon called *the apostasy;* and, if Revelation is the kind of book it is devoutly believed to be by this writer, there is no way for that apostasy to have been omitted from its pages. Where are *the eyes* of those scholars who can write a whole commentary on Revelation and never even mention it? What kind of astigmatism can be blind to the plainest references to it, and what kind of deafness is it that cannot hear the thunder of these middle chapters of Revelation?" (1979, p. 290).

CHAPTER 11
THE BATTLE OF ARMAGEDDON

Premillennialism is the dogma that Christ must return to the earth before he commences an alleged 1,000-year reign from Jerusalem. Dispensationalism is the notion that all of history is divided into seven ages (dispensations), which supposedly correspond to the days of the creation week – the seventh "age" being the millennial reign of Jesus. Almost every time there is a disturbance in the Middle East, voices of hysteria assert that the "battle of Armageddon" is imminent.

A recent example of the "prophetic" confusion in connection with Armageddon is the revised version of John F. Walvoord's book, **Armageddon, Oil and the Middle East Crisis**. For many years Walvoord was a Professor of Systematic Theology at the Dallas Theological Seminary; he now serves as Chancellor of that institution. Promotion for the book asserts that the world stage is set for a showdown in the Middle East. Walvoord argues that the recent conflict in the Persian Gulf fulfills conditions "exactly as the Bible anticipates in its prophecies of the end of time." The first printing of this book issued 300,000 copies, and a $40,000 national marketing campaign was initiated. After the fall of the Soviet Union, however, these books were dumped on the market at a fraction of the original price. Little wonder! Russia was supposed to be one of the super powers in the Armageddon conflict. The whole millennial scheme is without merit.

Does the Bible speak of the "battle of Armageddon"? If so, what is it? And when is it supposed to occur? Armageddon [literally, Har-Magedon] is specifically mentioned but once in the Scriptures. A passage in the book of Revelation states: "And they gathered them together into the place which is called in Hebrew Har-Magedon" (16:16). Before one is prepared to consider the possible meaning of "Armageddon," he must first understand something of the nature and design of the book of Revelation as a whole.

A Symbolic Book of Hope

Although we discussed some of these matters earlier in this book (Chapter 1), we feel compelled to review a few points before considering of the meaning of Armageddon. The book of Revelation is a highly symbolic book, as evidenced by both the introduction, and the type of material it contains. It is affirmed that Christ "signified" the message by his angel unto his servant John (1:1). "The Greek verb carries the idea of figurative representation. Strictly speaking it means to make known by some sort of sign ... it is admirably suited to the symbolic character of the book. This should warn the reader not to expect a literal presentation of future history, but a symbolic portrayal of that which must yet come to pass" (Mounce, p. 65). Thus, the book is filled with symbols – like blood, wine, harlot, gold, white robes, etc.

Again we must remind ourselves as to why the Lord chose these graphic figures through which to convey the instruction of the document. Biblical symbolism frequently served a two-fold purpose. First, "signs" could reveal truths, in a dramatic way, to those who were initiated in the meaning of the word-pictures. Second, these truths could be concealed from those who would abuse the information, had they access to it.

Compare, for example, Jesus' use of parables in the presence of the Jewish leaders (Mt. 13:13f). Therefore, this symbolic terminology (also called "apocalyptic" language) was employed generally by inspired writers to "smuggle" messages of hope to the Lord's people in times of great danger.

The book of Revelation is a proclamation of victory. We must mention again that one of the key words in the narrative is "overcome" (see the chapter on "Word Patterns"). It is a fact admitted by all that this book was written in a time of severe and widespread persecution. The object of the writing was thus to assure the followers of Christ of the ultimate and complete defeat of God's enemies, and the glorious triumph of the Christian religion.

This word of consolation was couched in the imagery of the Old Testament Scriptures. As we indicated earlier, Westcott and Hort's **Greek New Testament** lists over five hundred references and allusions from the Old Testament in the book of Revelation. The primitive Christians, being familiar with the Old Testament writings, would understand the symbols, hence, be sustained. Their enemies would not grasp the message. This technique surely spared the Christians from some persecution.

Any view of the book of Revelation that fails to recognize its highly symbolic nature – that seeks to literalize its images, is doomed to absolute failure! And this is the cardinal error of the dispensational premillennialists.

What Is Armageddon?

As noted earlier, the solitary biblical reference to "Armageddon" occurs near the end of Revelation 16. This awesome chapter records the pouring out of seven bowls of God's wrath into the earth (vs. 1). The bowls of wrath are in the form of plagues (sores, blood, fire, frogs), reminiscent of the Exodus plagues. They are designed to be universal, strictly punitive, and final. Leon Morris says: "They point us to God's overthrow of all that is evil" (p. 192).

In connection with the sixth bowl, John writes in Revelation 16:13-16, "And I saw coming out of the mouth of the dragon, and out of the mouth of the beast, and out of the mouth of the false prophet, three unclean spirits, as it were frogs: for they are spirits of demons, working signs; which go forth unto the kings of the whole world, to gather them together unto the war of the great day of God, the Almighty. (Behold, I come as a thief. Blessed is he that watcheth, and keepeth his garments, lest he walk naked, and they see his shame.) And they gathered them together into the place which is called in Hebrew Har-Magedon."

Surely even the most immature exegete ought to be able to discern the figures employed within this context. Are literal frogs literally going to come from the literal mouths of literal creatures to literally engage in battle on the literal plain of Megiddo? I would assume that even modern millennialists do not believe that the battle of Armageddon will be fought by frogs. The theory sort of "croaks" right there! Moreover, the plain of Megiddo is only about twenty miles long by fourteen miles wide. That is much too small to accommodate a battle of the magnitude (hundreds of millions of soldiers) demanded by modern dispensational writers.

What is the significance of the expression "Har-Magedon"? While recent New Testament criticism has debated the meaning of the term, Professor Eberhard Nestle says: "Upon the whole, to find an allusion here to Megiddo is still the most probable explanation" (p. 305). "The fact that the tell [hill] of Megiddo was about 70 feet high in John's day, and was in the vicinity of [the] Carmel Range, justifies the use of Hebrew *har*, used loosely in the Old Testament for 'hill' and 'hill country' ..." (Sheriffs, p. 505).

It needs to be recognized that in speaking of Armageddon (i.e., the mountain of Megiddo), the apostle John is *not* alluding to a *literal* place. The use of geographical points to emphasize spiritual truths is a common biblical phenomenon. Consider, for example, the word "hell" (Grk. *gehenna*). The Greek *gehenna* relates to the Hebrew *gehinnom*, which was the Valley of Hinnom just south of Jerusalem. In Old Testament times, when the Jews became involved in idolatry, they offered their children as burnt sacrifices there (2 Kgs. 16:3; 21:6). Later, because of its connection with pain, weeping, and burning (Hinnom, as the city dump, was continuously on fire), *gehenna* became a symbol for the final punishment of hell. Certainly it would be absurd to contend that on the Day of Judgment, the wicked will be cast into the literal Valley of Hinnom near Jerusalem!

Similarly, and characteristically, John frequently uses places as symbols for concepts. So Zion (14:1), or Jerusalem (21:2), are symbols of God's spiritual city, the church. Babylon signifies apostasy, and all that is opposed to God (14:8). Egypt and Sodom (11:8) represent oppression and wickedness, and the Euphrates (16:12) was symbolic of the point of origin of (spiritual) Israel's enemies, etc. It is within such a reference frame that "mountain of Megiddo" is likewise used.

The history of Megiddo is interesting. It is the earth's most famous battlefield. J.L. Hurlbut declared that "more battles have been fought on this plain than on any other in the world" (1954b, p. 15).

A number of famous Old Testament conflicts occurred there. It was renowned for the victories of Deborah and Barak over the Canaanites (Jdgs. 4:15,16), and of Gideon over the Midianites

(Jdgs. 7). Josiah was also killed in battle there (2 Kgs. 23:29).

"It is not unlikely," says Morris, "that the deliverance under Deborah is regarded as setting the pattern. Then Sisera had 900 chariots of iron (Jdgs. 4:13), but in Israel there was scarce a shield or spear among 40,000 (Jdgs. 5:8). Israel's position was completely hopeless. But when the battle was joined, 'the Lord routed Sisera and all his chariots and all his army' (Jdgs. 4:15 RSV). So will it be at the last day. However strong the forces of evil may appear, and however hopeless the position of those of good, God will win the victory. He will resoundingly overthrow the evil" (p. 200). And so, "The old battleground becomes the symbol of the decisive struggle, it is raised in meaning: it is a type, not a locality" (Carpenter, p. 609).

While some would identify the pouring out of God's wrath in Revelation 16 (including Armageddon) with the destruction of Jerusalem, or perhaps with the cessation of Roman persecution at the time of Constantine, it is more likely that Armageddon is used as a symbol of "the final overthrow of all the forces of evil by an almighty God" (Morris, p. 200). Professor Russel B. Jones says: "We seem to be on safe ground when we understand the ancient battlefield at Megiddo as a type of the final stand of the enemies of righteousness against the Lord at His appearing" (p. 88). Again, Mounce notes: "... Har-Magedon is symbolic of the final overthrow of all the forces of evil by the might and power of God" (p. 302). All of these factors surely lead to the conclusion that Armageddon is not a literal conflict.

It is important to observe that Revelation 16 actually says nothing about the battle of Armageddon taking place at that point. There, the forces are merely gathered together, awaiting "the war of the great day of God, the Almighty" when he comes "as a thief" (16:14-15). Note: the great day of God is "the day

Chapter 11: The Battle of Armageddon

of God's final judgment" (Arndt & Gingrich, p. 347), at which time the earth will be destroyed (2 Pet. 3:12). Moreover, the expression "come as a thief" is repeatedly employed in connection with Christ's second coming (Mt. 24:42,43; 1 Thes. 5:2; 2 Pet. 3:10).

The battle scene itself is pictured in Revelation 19:11-16. "And I saw the heaven opened; and behold a white horse, and he that sat thereon called Faithful and True; and in righteousness he doth judge and make war. And his eyes are a flame of fire, and upon his head are many diadems; and he hath a name written which no one knoweth but he himself. And he is arrayed in a garment sprinkled with blood: and his name is called The Word of God. And the armies which are in heaven followed him upon white horses, clothed in fine linen, white and pure. And out of his mouth proceedeth a sharp sword, that with it he should smite the nations; and he shall rule them with a rod of iron: and he treadeth the winepress of the fierceness of the wrath of God, the Almighty. And he hath on his garment and on his thigh a name written, King of kings and Lord of lords."

Concerning this remarkable description, the following observations are in order: First, the one coming from heaven is clearly Christ, the Word (Jn. 1:1, 14), and the white horse is a symbol of his victorious conquest. Second, he is coming to judge and make war. But judgment will take place at his second coming (Mt. 25:31ff); hence, his war against the enemies of Jehovah will occur at that time. Third, the Lord smites the rebellious nations with a sharp sword that proceeds out of his mouth. Elsewhere, Paul shows that at the time of his "coming" (Grk. *parousia* – a technical term for the Lord's final coming in judgment), Jesus Christ will slay His foes "with the breath of his mouth," and bring them to naught (2 Thes. 2:8).

In summation, our argument is arranged logically as follows:

(1) The battle of Armageddon will occur when Christ comes to judge (Rev. 16:16; 19:11).

(2) But he will judge at his second coming.

(3) The battle of Armageddon will thus take place at the second coming of Christ.

(1) The Armageddon war will take place when Jesus destroys his enemies with the breath of his mouth.

(2) But such will occur at his coming.

(3) Therefore, Armageddon is the punishment inflicted by Christ at his second coming.

Conclusion

The dispensational view of the battle of Armageddon is totally false. It contains not the slightest support in the Scriptures. Rather, it is grounded upon a novel and relatively recent (about a century ago) scheme of theological presuppositions. It is buttressed by an erroneous exegetical system which completely ignores the obvious symbolism of the book of Revelation and crudely literalizes its pictures. It is part of a doctrine that reflects in many ways upon the integrity of the Word of God, hence, must be rejected.

We have nothing to fear of an impending political Armageddon. However, all who are not in Christ (Gal. 3:26, 27), or who are unfaithful to the Lord (2 Cor. 11:2, 3), had best prepare against the awful day of spiritual Armageddon!

CHAPTER 12

THE THOUSAND-YEAR REIGN OF CHRIST

Near the end of the book of Revelation (20:1-6), the inspired apostle gloriously speaks of those who "lived, and reigned with Christ a thousand years" (4). This is the only portion of the entire Bible that addresses a "one thousand year reign" of Jesus Christ, and yet this context has become what George Murray called "the very citadel and bulwark of premillennial eschatology" (p. 175). An entire system of "end time" events has been constructed upon these scant, half-dozen verses. But, as one scholar has observed:

"In regard to a book so enigmatical, it were presumptuous to speak with any degree of dogmatism, but the uniform absence of the idea of the millennium from the eschatological teaching of the New Testament elsewhere ought to render the exegete cautious before affirming its presence here" (Vos, p. 987).

The word "millennium" derives from two Latin terms – *mille*, denoting a thousand, and *annum*, a year. The term thus signifies a thousand years. Theologically, the word owes its origin to the references in Revelation 20, where Christ is said to reign for 1,000 years. There are several religious viewpoints connected with the word "millennium."

Postmillennialism holds there will be a long period (c. 1,000 years) of gospel success, wherein millions will be converted; this will be a sort of "golden era," just before the return of Christ. Hence, the second coming is supposed to be after (*post*) this millennial period. This theory, first advocated by Daniel Whitby

(1638-1726), was entertained by some of the preachers in the early American restoration movement.

Amillennialism (meaning, "no millennium") contends that there will not be any literal 1,000-year era of peace, nor will Jesus return to the earth to reign from Jerusalem, etc. The 1,000 years, as with numerous other numbers in Revelation, is seen as a symbol for a spiritual truth. This viewpoint most consistently accords with all other New Testament data regarding the second coming of Christ.

Premillennialism holds that Jesus will return to earth before he commences a 1,000-year reign on David's throne in Palestine. The heretic, Cerinthus (fl. c. A.D. 100) may have been the first one to advocate a form of this doctrine. Eusebius, quoting Caius, says:

"But Cerinthus, by means of revelations which he pretended were written by a great apostle, also falsely pretended to wonderful things, as if they were showed him by angels, asserting, that after the resurrection there would be an earthly kingdom of Christ, and that the flesh, i.e. men, again inhabiting Jerusalem, would be subject to desires and pleasures. Being also an enemy to the divine Scriptures, with a view to deceive men, he said that there would be a space of a thousand years for celebrating nuptial festivals" (Book III, Chapter, XXVIII).

Dispensationalism, which we will discuss momentarily, is the most radical expression of premillennialism. Premillennialism, in all its forms, is fraught with great difficulty; it seriously contradicts the Bible in numerous ways (see the author's booklet, **Premillennialism – A System of Infidelity**). For an excellent survey of millennial ideas throughout Christian history, one should consult the commentary on the book of Revelation by James D. Strauss (pp. 282-292; see also Lee, pp. 808-814).

Chapter 12: The Thousand-Year Reign of Christ

As mentioned earlier, it is very foolish to attempt a forced harmony between the figurative elements of Revelation 20:1-6, and the dispensational or premillennial theories, because these views regarding the reign of Christ conflict with the Scriptures in many particulars. The famous Presbyterian scholar, Charles Hodge, made this point.

"It is a sound rule in the interpretation of Scripture that obscure passages should be so explained as to make them agree with those that are plain. It is unreasonable to make the symbolic and figurative language of prophecy and poetry the rule by which to explain the simple didactic prose language of the Bible. It is no less unreasonable that a multitude of passages should be taken out of their natural sense to make them accord with a single passage of doubtful import" (p. 842).

It may be safely said that were it not for the first half-dozen verses in Revelation 20, no one would have dreamed of the notion of a 1,000-year reign of Christ upon this earth. As one writer observes:

"It is admitted, on all hands, that this doctrine, if contained in the Scriptures at all, is found in this one passage only. It is not pretended that there is, in any other place, a direct affirmation that this will literally occur, nor would the advocates for that opinion undertake to show that it is fairly implied in any other part of the Bible. But it is strange, not to say improbable, that the doctrine of the literal resurrection of the righteous, a thousand years before the wicked, should be announced in one passage only" (Barnes, 1954, pp. 428, 429).

Before we discuss Revelation 20:1ff, setting forth possible solutions to the symbols of this chapter – which, at least, are consistent with the overall doctrinal program of the Bible, perhaps it would be wise to mention, and eliminate, two erroneous theories – believed by many, but so at variance with Bible truth: (a) realized eschatology and, (b) the dispensational or premillennial concept.

Revelation 20 and Realized Eschatology

Realized eschatology is commonly known as the A.D. 70 doctrine. It alleges that all Bible prophecy was fulfilled by A.D. 70 when Jerusalem was destroyed. This theory contends *that the millennium was that period between the time of the cross and the destruction of Jerusalem.* Here is what the leader of the current movement says: "Equating the millennium with the interim period between the cross/Pentecost beginning point and the A.D. 70 point of consummation agrees with the eschatological time frame of the Gospel and Epistles" (King, p. 212).

According to this notion, the "thousand years" of Revelation 20 symbolizes a mere *forty-year* span – between A.D. 30 and 70! It stretches one's imagination to understand how the number 1,000 can symbolize forty. Such a view is at odds with a basic pattern concerning the symbolic use of numbers. The use of definite round numbers is frequently designed to convey the concept of the indefinite – i.e., from the lesser to the greater (Smith, 1939, pp. 2158, 2159). Thus forgiving another person seventy times seven means forgiving *limitlessly* (Mt. 18:22). The expression 10,000 times 10,000 signifies a *numberless* multitude (Rev. 5:11). But 1,000 does not suggest *forty!*

Besides, the whole theory of realized eschatology is contrary to dozens of clear scriptural truths (see Jackson, 1990a). And so, let us give our attention to the more popular and formidable dogma of dispensationalism.

CHAPTER 12: THE THOUSAND-YEAR REIGN OF CHRIST

Revelation 20 and Dispensationalism

The following points of doctrine are components of dispensational theology.

(1) Millennialists contend that Christ came to earth for the purpose of setting up his kingdom (actually, a re-establishment of the Old Testament regime); since, however, he was surprised by the rejection of the Jews, he did not inaugurate the kingdom plan. Rather, as an "after-thought," he set up the church instead. Supposedly, the "kingdom" will be established when Jesus returns to earth.

This concept is riddled with error. (a) Christ was not *surprisingly* rejected by the Jews. His rejection had been prophesied centuries earlier (Psa. 118:22). (b) He did not *postpone* the kingdom; first century Christians were citizens of that divine regime (Jn. 3:5; Col. 1:13; Rev. 1:9). (c) The church was not an *afterthought*. It was a vital element in God's "eternal purpose" (Eph. 3:10, 11). (d) The coming of Christ will not *commence* the earthly kingdom; it will terminate it (cf. 1 Cor. 15:24).

(2) Dispensationalists contend that since returning to heaven, the Bridegroom (Christ) has been tarrying, but "signs" (especially Matthew 24) indicate that his return is imminent. There is no truth to this claim. The signs of Matthew 24 had to do with the impending destruction of Jerusalem, not the second coming of Christ. Verse 34 of the chapter clearly establishes this point (see Kik, pp. 1-8).

(3) The "first stage" of the Lord's coming is supposed to be a secret return, called "the Rapture." The living saints will be caught up to be with Jesus in the air, and the righteous dead will be raised from their graves. But there is no evidence that there will be a Rapture; this is a figment of someone's theological imagination (see Appendix I).

(4) It is claimed that the Rapture will trigger the "Tribulation Period." Allegedly, this is a span of seven years – equally divided into three and one-half year segments. In the first half, it is argued, the Jewish temple will be rebuilt, the law of Moses (with its animal sacrifices) will be re-instituted, and prosperity will reign. The latter half of the Tribulation Period is supposed to be one of bloody conflict – the Antichrist leading his forces against the Lord – culminated by the battle of Armageddon (see the chapter on "Armageddon").

Again, the error is manifold. (a) There is no "seven year" tribulation period specified in the Scriptures. (b) The Bible nowhere indicates that the Mosaic system (with its temple, sacrifices, etc.) will be revived. That is blasphemy. Paul argued that the law of Moses has been *permanently* abrogated – such is the force of the perfect tense verbal form "hath taken" in Colossians 2:14.

(5) After the Battle of Armageddon, according to dispensationalism, Jesus will come again (this would be his *third* coming). Yet see Hebrews 9:28 – which indicates that the Lord's final coming is the "second" one. At this time, so goes the theory, Christ will commence his earthly reign of 1,000 years – called the millennium. It is this final point that we must address in this chapter.

Millennialism: Missing Elements

Does Revelation 20 teach that Christ is going to reign for 1,000 years on David's throne from the city of Jerusalem? If it does, there is something very strange about the narrative – most all of the key components of the millennial theory are conspicuously absent from this context. Let us look carefully at this portion of scripture.

"And I saw an angel coming down out of heaven, having the

Chapter 12: The Thousand-Year Reign of Christ

key of the abyss and a great chain in his hand. And he laid hold on the dragon, the old serpent, which is the Devil and Satan, and bound him for a thousand years, and cast him into the abyss, and shut it, and sealed it over him, that he should deceive the nations no more, until the thousand years should be finished: after this he must be loosed for a little time.

"And I saw thrones, and they sat upon them, and judgment was given unto them: and I saw the souls of them that had been beheaded for the testimony of Jesus, and for the word of God, and such as worshipped not the beast, neither his image, and received not the mark upon their forehead and upon their hand; and they lived, and reigned with Christ a thousand years. The rest of the dead lived not until the thousand years should be finished. This is the first resurrection. Blessed and holy is he that hath part in the first resurrection: over these the second death hath no power; but they shall be priests of God and of Christ, and shall reign with him a thousand years" (20:1-6).

Now, reflect upon the following facts.

First, there is no mention in this context of the Rapture, the Tribulation Period, the restoration of Judaism, the Antichrist, or even the second coming of Christ.

Second, nothing is stated in this section regarding Jerusalem, David's throne, the kingdom of Christ, or the Lord's presence upon the earth.

Is it not strange that the vital ingredients of the dispensational scheme are not even remotely alluded to within this narrative? Put this segment of Revelation 20 under the microscope, sift it through a strainer, and still you will not find the coveted components. And yet, many people take for granted that these elements are found in Revelation 20 – but they are not! What, then, does Revelation 20 teach?

A Survey of Revelation 20

The twentieth chapter of the Apocalypse is one of the most thrilling, encouraging portions of the entire New Testament. It divides itself into four natural segments: (a) the binding of Satan (1-3); (b) the victorious reign of the faithful (4-6); (c) the final struggle and defeat of the devil (7-10); and, (d) the Day of Judgment (11-15). The chapter may be summarized as follows.

John saw an angel descending from heaven with a great chain. Satan was bound with the chain and cast into a pit where he was consigned to remain for 1,000 years. As a consequence of this event, judgment was granted to those faithful martyrs who had neither worshiped the beast nor his image. These martyrs were said to partake of a resurrection; further, they lived and reigned with Christ for a thousand years. Satan was then loosed to make a final attempt to war against the saints, but he and his unholy allies lose the conflict and ultimately are banished to torment. All of the dead are then ushered before the great throne of God for final judgment.

It is immediately apparent that this portion of Revelation, as with the balance of the book, is highly symbolic. The description is punctuated with figures of speech. There is a key, a chain, a dragon or serpent, a pit, a thousand years, thrones, a beast, marks on foreheads and hands, and a resurrection. It is certainly a novel view, to say the least, to contend that a figurative serpent was figuratively bound with a figurative chain, and figuratively thrown into a figurative pit, which was figuratively locked with a figurative key, for *a literal thousand years!*

Even if one does not fully comprehend the fullness of the symbolism involved, surely he can see the figurative nature of the language. It is an absurd error to literalize a solitary feature of this symbolic narrative.

The One-Thousand Year Reign

As has been demonstrated above, the dispensational view of Revelation cannot be correct. There is no evidence whatever that this context prophesies of a time when Christ will return to the earth for the purpose of establishing a theocratic kingdom reminiscent of David's regime in Old Testament history.

To what, then, does the 1,000-year reign refer? There are several possible ideas that have been suggested by scholarly, non-premillennial writers. As we consider these concepts, remember this – whatever view one entertains, it must be one that is consistent with the overall teaching of the Bible. The dispensational or premillennial view is not in harmony with basic Bible doctrine. And so, even if one is unable to confidently affirm what the 1,000-year reign signifies, he may with certainty know what it is *not*. And it is not an earthly reign to be ushered in by the Lord's second coming.

One thing is clear – a consistent mode of interpretation, both of this context and the book of Revelation as a whole, will establish this fact – the "thousand years" is not a literal period of history. The numeral "thousand" is used more than twenty times in the book of Revelation, and *not once is it employed in a literal sense*. It is not any more sensible to argue that Christ is going to reign 1,000 literal years, than it is to urge that only 144,000 people will be in heaven (cf. Rev. 7; 14; see also Chapter 7 of this work). The "thousand" is a symbol. W.W. Milligan comments: "'[T]he thousand years mentioned in the passage express no period of time .... They embody an idea; and that idea, whether applied to the subjugation of Satan or to the triumph of the saints is the idea of completeness or perfection. Satan is bound for a thousand years; that is, he is completely bound. The saints reign for a thousand years; that is, they are introduced into a state of perfect and glorious victory" (p. 913). What, then, do the "thousand years" signify?

Reign of Martyrs

Some expositors have argued that the millennium is a symbol for the completeness of that rest which Christ provides for those who have died for their faith. They would view the "thousand years" as a descriptive of the intermediate state of the believers after death (Winters, p. 231), or perhaps simply "the victory of the martyred saints" (Ladd, p. 390).

Robert Mounce toys with a similar view. He writes: "A careful reading of the millennial passage (vss. 1-10) will show that it is perhaps limited to the resurrected martyrs alone, and that it contains no specific indication that their reign with Christ takes place on earth or that it necessarily follows the second coming of Christ ..." (p. 351). Mounce argues that "John taught a literal millennium, but its essential meaning may be realized in something other than a temporal fulfillment" (p. 359).

The Gospel Age

There are many who believe that the millennium is "co-extensive with the Gospel Age" (Jones, p. 109). Another scholar, William Cox, says: "The kingdom – in its present phase – and the millennium are practically, if not altogether, synonymous terms" (p. 180).

A 3rd century theologian, Tyconius, "taught that the thousand years of Revelation 20:4-6 refer to the present age and to those who are reborn through baptism: the physical resurrection is in the future. The millennial rule of Christ extends from his passion to his second coming" (Ford, p. 834). Tyconius influenced Augustine, who argued that the millennium began with the incarnation of Jesus and was fully realized in the experience of the earthly church.

The late Roy H. Lanier, Sr., a respected and beloved brother, felt that the thousand year span "is that period of duration, however short or long it may be, from the binding of Satan and the coronation of Jesus on David's throne on Pentecost after his resurrection to the destruction of Satan and his followers on the day of judgment" (p. 232). Howard Winters also adopted this position (p. 227), as did Burton Coffman (1979, p. 465). According to this view, the "first resurrection" (20:5) would refer either to the "new birth" (Cox, p. 166), or to the translation of souls to be with Christ (Lanier, p. 234).

An Era of Victory

Another view – one which appears to accord better with all other facts – suggests that the "thousand years" is a symbolic description of the revival of Christianity from an era of bloody persecution. Earlier in the Revelation, John viewed the "souls" of the martyrs "underneath the altar" crying, "How long, O Master, the holy and true, doth thou not judge and avenge our blood on them that dwell on the earth?" (6:9-11). Now, however, in chapter 20, the apostle sees those "souls" on "thrones," reigning with Christ.

For a while, Christianity appeared to have been buried in tribulation; ultimately, though, it emerged. It was, figuratively speaking, "resurrected." Compare John's statement, "This is the first resurrection" (5). This type of symbolism is not uncommon in apocalyptic literature. The Hebrew deliverance from Babylonian captivity is figuratively depicted as a resurrection in the book of Ezekiel – in the prophet's vision of the valley of dry bones (Ezek. 37). See also Isaiah 26:18 and Romans 11:15 for similar usages of this type of language.

And so, the "first resurrection" (of vs. 5) would represent the victorious triumphs of the persecuted saints. This appears to be borne out by the fact that the apostle says that "the second death hath no power" over these reigning souls (6). However, back in an earlier portion of the book, *this same promise* was made regarding those who "overcome" (2:11). Thus, "resurrection" may simply be a figure of speech for "overcoming." The "thousand years" aspect may suggest that their victory was *complete*, or it may hint of a relatively longer period of prosperity, as compared with a more abbreviated time of persecution (Roberts, p. 171).

If one interprets the "millennium" as a symbol of the church's victory over her enemies, the specific application of this concept will depend upon the general view one entertains regarding the book of Revelation as a whole.

For instance, the *Early Preterist* view (see Introduction) would view this scene as a picture of the church's victory over the persecuting forces of Judaism. Foy Wallace, in his commentary on Revelation, argued this theory.

On the other hand, the *Late Preterist* concept sees the narrative as a description of Christianity's triumph over the Jewish, and then Roman, persecutions during the early centuries of the church's history. This is the thrust of J.W. Roberts' commentary, and similarly that of Jim McGuiggan. McGuiggan says that "[a]ll the historical events dealt with (prophesied of), in the book, have been fulfilled!" (p. 12).

We must point out, however, that this view of the Apocalypse dates only from the early 17th century. Apparently it was first conceived by a Spanish Jesuit priest by the name of Alcasar, and it has been happily embraced by Catholic theologians who are "anxious to avert the application of the Apocalyptic prophecies from the papacy" (McClintock & Strong, VIII p. 259). Some Protestant interpreters, and not a few of our own brethren, have accepted this view, without, perhaps, being aware of its origin or flaws.

The *Idealist* theory would suggest that the millennium merely represents any victory that the people of God enjoy over their opposing enemies. Again, we emphasize that, in our view, this explanation is much too vague. It fails to do justice to the prophetic thrust of the book. The principle, of course, has value for all time, but the book must not be divorced from history.

Finally, many writers in the *Historical* school of thought, as reflected in the works of Barnes, Clarke, our own John T. Hinds (Gospel Advocate series), and others, would see the millennium in terms of the church's conquest over its persecutors (both pagan and papal), which results in a period of gospel prosperity prior to the Lord's return. During this time, the "souls" of the martyrs are "resurrected" [not literally, for a "soul" cannot be literally resurrected] i.e., *resurrected in the cause of truth* as it exerts its benevolent influence, generally unimpeded, in an evil world. Of this "millennium," Clarke says:

"I am satisfied that this period should not be taken literally. It may signify that there shall be a long and undisturbed state of Christianity; and so universally shall the Gospel spirit prevail, that it will appear as if Christ reigned upon earth; which will in effect be the case, because his Spirit shall rule in the hearts of men; and in this time the martyrs are represented as living again; their testimony being revived, and the truth for which they died, and which was confirmed by their blood, being now everywhere prevalent" (p. 1055).

Albert Barnes observes that the "resurrection" alluded to in 20:5 is not designated as a resurrection because it resembles the final resurrection in every particular; rather, it merely suggests "a coming to life again" (1954, p. 426), which would be accomplished when "the *principles* of the martyrs" are "revived and would live, as if the dead were being raised up" (1954, p. 430). This would be accomplished in future generations by those who embraced and fearlessly proclaimed the primitive gospel. Barnes' discussion of this topic is excellent.

I must add this comment. There is a tendency today, especially among younger preachers, to ridicule Barnes, Clarke, and other commentators of an earlier age. The fact of the matter is, the scholarship of some of those men was vastly superior to their modern critics.

David Brown, who served as Professor of Divinity at Free Church College, Aberdeen, and who was a major contributor to the famous Jamieson, Fausset, & Brown **Bible Commentary** series, authored an important volume titled: **Christ's Second Coming – Will It Be Premillennial?** (in which he answered that query negatively). In this work, Professor Brown wrote an extended section, involving nine major arguments, in which he demonstrated that the "first resurrection" of the millennial period is a *figurative* resurrection, not a literal one during which Christ is physically present on earth (pp. 217-242). This discussion is well worth reading for those who wish to explore this matter in greater detail. This latter view of Revelation 20 has much to commend it. We are not suggesting that it is without difficulties. On the whole, however, it is the conviction of this writer that it explains all of the relevant data better than any other viewpoint.

Great Lessons from Revelation Chapter 20

Aside from the difficult spots in Revelation 20, there are many tremendous lessons, practical and meaningful, which can be gleaned from this powerful chapter. Some of these are as follows:

(a) Satan's influence is not unrestrained in this evil world. With the coming of Christ, the inauguration of his law, and the unimpeded dispersal of the Holy Scriptures around the world, the devil's activities have been bound considerably. The influence of Christianity has been phenomenal (cf. Acts 17:6).

(b) Suffering is not purposeless. It affords man the opportunity to exhibit the noblest qualities of which he is capable. In suffering as Christians, we glorify God (1 Pet. 4:16).

(c) Christianity is a cause worth dying for, because "judgment" was given to those beheaded for the testimony of Jesus (4).

(d) Faithfulness pays. Those who worshiped neither the beast nor his image, nor received his mark, reigned with Jesus (4, 6).

(e) Satan, the arch-enemy of man, will be banished to hell ultimately (10). This opponent of God, who has caused such woe in the world, will not escape his destiny.

(f) Hell is a place of eternal, conscious torment. Satan is tormented for ever and ever; but torment implies consciousness. Hence, there is conscious punishment forever. Since the Bible teaches that wicked humans will also suffer this fate (Mt. 25:41, 46; 2 Thes. 1:9; Mk. 9:48), one may draw certain deductions as to the nature of their punishment as well.

(g) There will be a great day of judgment upon which all, both great and small, will appear before the Ruler of the Universe to give account for their works according to divine law (11-13). There are those who think judgment is a joke, but Jehovah will have the last laugh (cf. Psa. 2:4).

(h) On that great day "death and Hades" will give up the dead. That is, the grave will surrender the body and the Hadean realm will give up the soul. Then the two – immortal body (1 Cor. 15:52) and incorruptible spirit (1 Pet. 3:4), will then be assigned their eternal relationships (cf. Mt. 10:28).

CHAPTER 13

A NEW HEAVENS AND A NEW EARTH

Near the end of the book of Revelation, the inspired apostle writes: "And I saw a new heaven and a new earth: for the first heaven and the first earth are passed away; and the sea is no more" (21:1). To what does the expression "new heaven and a new earth" refer? Does it suggest that the present earth will be renovated, to serve as the eternal abiding place for the people of God? Many believe this concept.

Some are so enamored with this earth and its trappings that they apparently long to be here forever. Misunderstanding the nature of symbolic language (as in the passage cited above), they contend that the earth will be man's eternal domain. As we mentioned in an earlier chapter, the "Jehovah's Witnesses" argue that only 144,000 people will inhabit heaven; the remainder of the redeemed will live on God's "glorified earth." Others, adopting an equally erroneous viewpoint, have argued that all saints will live eternally on earth, and that God himself will come down and live with them. Robert Shank has written:

"Here is one of the most exciting truths in the Bible: God will come to earth to make his home among men! This is his plan and goal. He will bring heaven with him when he comes, of course, but the perspective here (the final perspective of the Bible) is earthward rather than heavenward. Earth has been the habitat of man, but God wants to live here too" (p. 294).

Robert Milligan, a restoration leader, taught that the earth would be renovated by fire on the judgment and that the New

Jerusalem would be on this planet (pp. 574-577). The foregoing notion appears to be common among denominational writers. Hendriksen says: "The universe is going to be gloriously rejuvenated and transformed. Remember: the same universe, but renewed!" (p. 239). This theory is not supported by solid, biblical exegesis.

The Fate of the Earth

There are several passages in the Bible which clearly indicate the temporal nature of the earth. Immediately after the Flood, Jehovah alluded to the temporary status of the earth when he said: "While the earth remaineth, seedtime and harvest, and cold and heat, and summer and winter, and day and night shall not cease" (Gen. 8:22). Jesus emphatically said: "Heaven [i.e., the material region beyond the earth] and earth shall pass away" (Mt. 24:35).

The writer of Hebrews, in contrasting the eternal Christ with the heavens and the earth, declares that the latter will "perish" (Heb. 1:11, 12). And Peter settles the matter forever when he states that "the heavens that now are, and the earth, by the same word have been stored up for fire ..." (2 Pet. 3:7). He goes on to affirm that "the heavens shall pass away with a great noise, and the elements shall be dissolved with fervent heat, and the earth and the works that are therein shall be burned up" (2 Pet. 3:10-12). For a discussion of the erroneous assertion that "burned up" merely means "discovered" (ASVfn), see my article elsewhere (1984, p. 347, 348).

Some allege the Bible teaches that the earth will exist forever. They contend that several passages in scripture teach this. Among these are Psalm 78:69; 104:5, and Ecclesiastes 1:4 – "... the earth abideth for ever." Within these verses, however, the Hebrew term *olam* is used. The word simply means "age-lasting."

Robert Girdlestone has observed that the word is qualified by the nature of the object to which it is applied. "When applied to things physical, it is used in accordance with the revealed truth that the heaven and earth shall pass away, and it is limited by this truth" (p. 317). The word merely suggests that the object under consideration will last as long as it is designed to last. The term is used of the Jewish passover (Ex. 12:14), and the Levitical priesthood (Num. 25:13) – both of which passed away with the abrogation of the Mosaic system. Thus, the earth will last only as long as God purposes, i.e., until time ends, but not into eternity.

The New Environment

What, then, is that "new heavens and a new earth," promised to the faithful both by Peter and John (2 Pet. 3:13; Rev. 21:1)? Consider the following facts.

(1) The new heavens and the new earth cannot be *literally* the heavens and earth of which we are now citizens. Otherwise, the Bible is in a state of contradiction. In both of the New Testament contexts in which the new heavens and new earth are mentioned, it is plainly affirmed that this present material universe is destined for total destruction. We have already alluded to 2 Peter 3:10ff; now we turn our attention to Revelation 21:1. John declares that "the first heaven and the first earth are passed away; and the sea is no more." In addition to this statement, John, in describing the Judgment scene, affirms: "... from whose [God's] face the earth and the heaven fled away; and there was found no place for them" (20:11). The meaning of this latter phrase is this – "they were completely destroyed" (Morris, p. 240).

(2) In logic there is a principle which states that things equal to the same thing are equal to each other. Consider this application: if it can be established that the faithful are to enter heaven,

and yet, it is at the same time affirmed that they shall live in a "new heavens and the new earth," it should reasonably follow that the two expressions represent the *same* state. Is it thus true that heaven is promised to faithful children of God? Indeed. Observe the following passages.

(a) Christ would have us rejoice when we are persecuted, for great is our reward in heaven (Mt. 5:12).

(b) We must lay up treasures in heaven, and not on earth (Mt. 6:19, 20). The two states are obviously not the same.

(c) Those who forsake all to follow Jesus are promised treasure in heaven (Mt. 19:21).

(d) When this earthly tabernacle (the present physical body) is dissolved, we will have a new abiding place "in the heavens" (2 Cor. 5:1).

(e) The obedient have their names written in heaven, which means they are "enrolled" there (Lk. 10:20; Heb. 12:23).

(f) When Christ ascended from the earth, he went to heaven (Mk. 16:19), but he went as a "forerunner" for us (Heb. 6:19, 20). And he "dedicated for us" that way (Heb. 10:20).

(g) The Bible teaches that there is "one hope" (Eph. 4:4) – not two (earth and heaven) – and that hope is laid up for us "in the heavens" (Col. 1:5). Yes, our inheritance is "reserved in heaven" for us (1 Pet. 1:4).

The Nature of Heaven

But what is heaven like? It should be noted that heaven, wherever it is, is not a *material* place. It is a "new" type of environment. That is the significance of the term "new" as a modifier of the "heavens" and "earth." The Greek word *kainos* denotes that which is qualitatively fresh. Heaven is *spiritual*.

There is a beautiful portrayal of heaven in the 21st and 22nd chapters of the book of Revelation. First, as previously indicated, it is represented as "a new heaven and a new earth" (21:1). The narrative contains a stirring description of those who will, and will not, dwell in that glorious state (21:6-8). There is a breathtaking picture of this happy realm of the redeemed, described figuratively as consisting of precious stones and pure gold (21:9-27). It is a place of perpetual day, without sin, sickness, sadness or death (4; 23-27; cf. 7:16-17; 22:3,15). One must ever keep in mind that John's visions consist of many symbols, the design of which is to represent the glory and beauty of heaven. It is surely a mistake to view these descriptives in a literal fashion as some have done. Note the erroneous statement of Thiessen: "There is abundant reason for holding that this is a literal city. It has foundations, gates, walls, and streets. It is a cube .... All these things indicate that this is a literal city" (1949, p. 517).

We now live in the flesh; in a material world. Our only perceptions, as gained from personal experience, are material in nature. Thus, we simply are not, at this present stage of our existence, prepared to clearly understand what heaven will actually be like. In this regard, it is a challenge to walk by faith, for we cannot walk by sight. Consequently, the Spirit has employed many figures of speech, consisting of precious material things, to convey to us the value of heaven.

Heaven is not a place of *physical* existence. Paul declared that "flesh and blood cannot inherit the kingdom of God" (1 Cor. 15:50). By way of contrast, the Moslem concept of heaven is quite physical. One writer has noted that a factor in the spread of Islam has been that "[e]veryone [Islamic warriors] who fell in battle with the unbelievers was destined to enter an immediate heaven of sensual delight" (Hurlbut, 1954a, p. 117-118).

Equally erroneous is the Mormon notion that the marriage

relationship obtains in heaven. Jesus plainly affirmed that "in the resurrection, they neither marry, nor are given in marriage" (Mt. 22:30). One preacher recently revealed his crassly carnalistic view of heaven by suggesting that his *dog* would be in that celestial state! Such false ideas as these have no basis in biblical fact.

It may be difficult to understand how we can enjoy heaven if there will be absolutely no physical pleasures there. We must remember, however, that all physical appetites wane with the passing of time. Heaven is an eternal state. Consequently, the bliss of that future existence will be adapted to us as we then will be, and not as we now are. This must necessarily be the case if we are to be *eternally* happy!

The Blessings of Heaven

Though we cannot fathom the intricacies of heaven from our current vantage point, surely we can appreciate some of the blessings of that state as set forth in the divine record.

(a) Heaven is a place of *rest* from earthly hardships. "Blessed are the dead who die in the Lord. From henceforth, yea saith the Spirit, that they may rest from their labors; for their works follow with them" (Rev. 14:13). "Let us therefore give diligence to enter into that rest" (Heb. 4:11).

(b) Heaven is a place of *reaping* (cf. Gal. 6:9). This earth is supposed to be a sphere of obedient activity wherein one lays up treasures to be finally enjoyed in heaven (Mt. 6:19). All who have faithfully worked in the interest of others here below, will be received by those friends into "the eternal tabernacles" above (Lk. 16:9). There will be a tremendous "reward" of satisfaction in knowing that we have helped to increase the population of heaven (cf. 1 Cor. 3:14).

(c) Heaven will be a place of *rejoicing*. Those who remain loyal to Christ will hear the Master say, "Well done, good and faithful servant ... enter thou into the joy of thy Lord" (Mt. 25:21). All who enter heaven will rejoice for the great victory they have won over the forces of evil (Rev. 12:11, 12; 19:7).

(d) Heaven will be a place of *righteousness*. "And there shall in no wise enter into it anything unclean, or he that makes an abomination and a lie: but only they that are written in the Lamb's book of life" (Rev. 21:27). "Without are the dogs, and the sorcerers, and the idolaters, and every one that loveth and maketh a lie" (22:15).

(e) Heaven will be a place of *responsibility*. The celestial realm will not be a domain of idle inactivity. There "his servants shall serve him" (Rev. 22:3). In one of his parables, Jesus told of ten servants who were each entrusted by their master with money to invest in trading. When they were finally called to account, each was rewarded with responsibility in direct proportion to the way in which he had used his ability (Lk. 19:16-19).

(f) Heaven will be a place of *reunion and recognition*. When the patriarchs died, they were "gathered to [their] people" (Gen. 25:8; 35:29). Both Jacob and David expected to be reunited with loved ones after death (Gen. 37:35; 2 Sam. 12:23). The Lord taught that we shall "sit down with Abraham, and Isaac, and Jacob, in the kingdom of heaven" (Mt. 8:11). Paul affirmed that those whom he had helped in their heavenward journey would be a source of joy at the time of the Lord's return (1 Thes. 2:19-20). This clearly implies future recognition. (For a more detailed discussion of this point, see: Jackson, 1987).

Surely with these great blessings ever before us, we will constantly renew our diligence to obtain this magnificent destiny.

APPENDIX I

DOES REVELATION SANCTION THE DOCTRINE OF "THE RAPTURE"?

Dispensationalists argue that the "rapture" of the church is prophesied in the book of Revelation. The Rapture Theory asserts that some seven years before Christ begins his millennial reign on earth, he will secretly and silently "snatch away" his saints to heaven. Advocates of this dogma contend that it is biblically based in 1 Thessalonians 4:14ff. There Paul speaks of believers being "caught up" to be with the Lord in the air (17). The fact is, however, this reference is an allusion to the second coming of Christ at the end of the world, and not to some mythical "rapture."

In Revelation 4:1, a heavenly voice beckons to John: "Come up hither ...." Supposedly, this is a reference to the rapture of the church. In the footnote of his Reference Bible, C.I. Scofield comments on this passage. "This call seems clearly to indicate the fulfillment of 1 Thes. 4:14-17. The word 'church' does not again occur in the Revelation till all is fulfilled."

So what? The word "church" does not occur in 2 Timothy, Titus, 1st Peter, 2nd Peter, 1st John, 2nd John, or Jude. What would such omissions indicate about the rapture? The mere absence of a word within a given context is no evidence at all. Moreover, the final mention of the church in Revelation does not refer to some heavenly, raptured organism; rather the term is plural, "churches" (22:16); it is employed of congregations in their individual, earthly capacity.

Alan Johnson, a premillennialist, confesses: "There is no good reason for seeing the invitation for John to come up into the opened heaven as a symbol of the rapture of the church" (p. 461). Robert Mounce agrees: "There is no basis for discovering a rapture of the church at this point" (p. 134).

The doctrine of the "rapture" became popular a few years ago when Hal Lindsey published his little book, **The Late Great Planet Earth**. He described the event as follows: "There I was, driving down the freeway and all of a sudden the place went crazy ... cars going in all directions ... and not one of them had a driver. I mean it was wild! I think we've got an invasion from outer space!" (pp. 124, 125). Lindsey's explanation for this frantic scene, as drawn from his overwrought imagination, is that these automobiles had been driven by Christians, who were suddenly and mysteriously caught up to be with the invisible Christ.

The word "rapture" is derived from the Latin *rapio*, which means "to seize" or "to snatch." Though this word is not in the Bible, dispensationalists claim the idea is found in First Thessalonians 4:17. There Paul speaks of the second coming of Christ; he declares that those living saints who witness the Lord's return will be "caught up" (*harpagesometha*) in the clouds to meet him. To use this context, though, as proof of a silent, secret return of Christ is – as Alexander Reese, a premillennialist, confessed – one of the sorriest attempts "in the whole history of freak exegesis" (quoted by Murray, p. 137). The "rapture" theory is contradicted by the following biblical facts.

(1) Christ's return will not be *invisible;* rather, it will be universally manifest. "For as the lightning cometh forth from the east, and is seen [from *phaino*, "to shine"] even unto the west; so [*houtos*, "in this manner"] shall be the coming [*parousia*] of

the Son of Man" (Mt. 24:27). As those early disciples "beheld" (*theaomai*, "to see, look at") Christ's departure to heaven, so in like manner (*tropos*, "in the same way") will he come again (Acts 1:11).

The Lord's coming will involve a "revelation" (*apokalupsis*, "to uncover") of his being (2 Thes. 1:7). At that time Christ will be "manifested" (*phaneroo*) – a term which, when employed in the passive voice (as in 1 Jn. 2:28), means to "show or reveal oneself, be revealed, appear to someone" (Arndt & Gingrich, p. 860). Moreover, as Jesus was visible during his first "appearing" (*epiphaneia*) on earth (2 Tim. 1:10), so will he be visible when he appears at his second coming (1 Tim. 6:14; 2 Tim. 4:1, 8; Tit. 2:13).

Finally, of his coming it is said that Jesus shall "appear" (*horao*, "become visible") a *second* time (Heb. 9:28). If the advocates of the rapture theory are correct, the Lord will not appear until his *third* coming! That's too many comings.

(2) Christ's coming will not be *inaudible;* rather, scripture indicates that the second advent will be accompanied by considerable sound phenomena. The Lord will descend from heaven with "a *shout*, with the *voice* of the archangel, and with the *trump* of God" (1 Thes. 4:16). This has been called the noisiest verse in the Bible. Too, when Jesus comes again, "the heavens shall pass away with a great noise" (2 Pet. 3:10). That hardly accords with the notion that the return of the Lord will be a silent, secret event.

The History of the Rapture Theory

The Rapture Theory is relatively recent. The idea appears to be traceable to a Pentecostal movement of the early 1800's – founded by Edward Irving (1792-1834). A recent writer says:

"The idea of a two-stage coming of Christ first came to a Scottish lass, Miss Margaret Macdonald of Port Glasgow, Scotland, while she was in a 'prophetic' trance" (Brinsmead, p. 28). Brinsmead quotes from a book, published in 1861, by Dr. Robert Norton, a member of the Irvingite group. This volume, titled **The Restoration of Apostles and Prophets: In the Catholic Apostolic Church** (p. 15), as quoted by Brinsmead, reads as follows:

"Marvelous light was shed upon Scripture, and especially on the doctrine of the second Advent, by the revived spirit of prophecy. In the following account by Miss M.M. – , of an evening during which the power of the Holy Ghost rested upon her for several successive hours, in mingled prophecy and vision, we have an instance; for here we first see the distinction between that final stage of the Lord's coming, when every eye shall see Him, and His prior appearing in glory to them that look for Him."

George Murray, in his excellent volume, **Millennial Studies**, has also quoted the renown Greek scholar, S.P. Tregelles, who, in 1864, wrote: "I am not aware that there was any definite teaching that there should be a Secret Rapture of the Church at a secret coming until this was given forth as an 'utterance' in Mr. Irving's church from what was then received as being the voice of the Spirit" (Murray, p. 138).

The Rapture Theory thus rests upon the same sort of basis as Shakerism (founder Ann Lee had visions and claimed to speak in seventy-two languages), Seventh-Day Adventism (Ellen White thought she took a trip to heaven), and Christian Science (Mary Baker Eddy's revelations told her there is no death).

The dispensational dogma, with all its peculiar elements (including the notion of a secret rapture), is at variance with the teaching of the Bible, and careful students of Holy Writ will reject it.

APPENDIX II

WHO IS PAUL'S "MAN OF SIN"?

In his first letter to the Christians in Thessalonica, Paul spoke of the return of Christ, and the glories associated therewith. Because some of these saints apparently misunderstood the instruction of that initial epistle, or had been influenced by false teaching, the apostle was constrained to write a second letter, attempting to correct the erroneous ideas entertained by the Thessalonians.

Apparently, there were heretics in the vicinity of Thessalonica who were advocating strange ideas regarding the Lord's return. Here is how Paul described that situation.

"Now we request you, brethren, with regard to the coming of our Lord Jesus Christ and our gathering together to Him, that you may not be quickly shaken from your composure or be disturbed either by a spirit or a message or a letter as if from us, to the effect that the day of the Lord has come" (2 Thes. 2:1, 2 NASB).

Notice that final clause, "the day of the Lord has come." It reflects a perfect tense form in the original language, and so may suggest that certain errorists of that day were alleging that the second coming had already occurred – somewhat as the advocates of realized eschatology do today. [Note: the proponents of the A.D. 70 doctrine (popularly known among churches of Christ as the Max King movement) allege that this passage implies that the second coming was to be an invisible, judgmental coming (i.e., in the destruction of Jerusalem); otherwise, these false teachers could never have gotten away with their assertion that the second coming had occurred already. Does that conclusion follow? It does not. It merely demonstrates that just as men then could be misled into believing that the Lord's coming was spiritual (rather than visible, literal), so folks can be equally deceived today – and some are, as evidenced by the King sect. For further study on this theme, see Jackson, 1990a.]

At any rate, Paul argued that the Lord could not have come, because "the falling away" must develop before the second coming transpires. Incidentally, no great apostate movement evolved between the time this letter was written c. A.D. 51, and A.D. 70, thus demonstrating, with a force equal to the apostle's original argument, that the second coming of Christ did not occur with the destruction of Jerusalem.

After laying this foundation, Paul continued his letter by describing the traits that would characterize that movement which he subsequently designates as "the man of sin." It is the purpose of this discussion to attempt an identification of this "man of sin."

Some may wonder: "What does this have to do with the book of Revelation?" Simply this: It is generally recognized that the "man of sin," as reflected in 2 Thessalonians, chapter 2, is the same force or movement as that described by Daniel as the "little horn" (chapter 7), and also the "beast" – especially the second beast (13:11ff) – in John's apocalyptic vision (see McClintock & Strong, I p. 254). Mason says: "It seems impossible to doubt that this great opponent [the man of sin] is the same as the 'Little Horn' of Daniel ..." (p. 167).

What are the identifying traits of the man of sin? We would suggest at this point that the student carefully read 2 Thessalonians 2:1-12. Read it several times, perhaps in different translations, to thoroughly familiarize yourself with the material. Having done so, we believe it is possible to isolate certain tell-tale qualities of this diabolical force, and so to work toward a solution as to the identity of the "man of sin." Consider the following factors.

Traits of the Man of Sin

(a) The man of sin is the ultimate result of "the falling away" from the faith (v. 3). The expression "falling away" translates the Greek term *apostasia*. Our English word "apostasy" is an anglicized form of this original term. In the Bible, the word is used of a departure from the religion ordained by God. As a noun, it is employed of leaving the Mosaic system (Acts 21:21), and, in this present passage, of defection from Christianity. The verbal form of the term is similarly used in 1 Timothy 4:1 (cf. Heb. 3:12). Note also that the noun is qualified by a definite article (*he apostasia*). A definite movement is in the apostle's prophetic vision.

(b) From a first-century vantage point, this sinister force was yet to be "revealed" (v. 3). This suggests that the movement had not evolved to the point where it could be identified definitely by the early saints. It awaited future development.

(c) This persecuting power was designated as "the man of sin" (v. 3), because sin is its "predominating quality" (Ellicott, p. 118). It [he] (referred to in both neuter and masculine genders – vss. 6, 7) is the "son of perdition" (v. 3), because its end is to be perdition, i.e., destruction by the Lord himself (v. 8). Finally, this opponent of God is called "the lawless one" (v. 8). This power has no regard for the law of God. One cannot but be reminded of that infamous "little horn" in Daniel's vision. "[H]e shall think to change the times and the law ..." (7:25).

(d) The man of sin opposes God and exalts himself against

all that is genuinely sacred (4). He feigns religiosity, but his true character reveals that he is diabolic. His activity is actually "according to the working of Satan" (v. 9).

(e) In some sense, the Man of Sin will "sit in the temple of God" (v. 4). The "temple" is not a reference to the Jewish house of worship. The Greek word is *naos*, used by Paul eight times. Never does he employ the term of the Jewish temple. In fact, after the death of Christ, the Jewish temple is never called the *temple of God* (Newton, p. 441). Rather it is used of the Christian's body (1 Cor. 6:19), or of the church as God's spiritual house (1 Cor. 3:16, 17; Eph. 2:21). The suggestion is this: This unholy being is viewed as a "church" character. The expression "sitteth" may hint of unparalleled arrogance (Ellicott, pp. 119, 120). Mason notes that the language describes the man of sin as attempting to exact "divine homage" from people (p. 169). Moreover, this son of perdition "sets himself forth as God." The present participle ("sets forth continually") reveals that this presumptive posture is characteristic of the man of sin. This person represents himself as God, either: (i) by making claims which belong only to deity; (ii) by receiving adoration reserved exclusively for God; or, (iii) by presuming prerogatives which only the Lord can implement. Clearly, the man of sin is an ecclesiastical character. Recall the description of John's lamb-like beast in Revelation 13:11ff.

(f) He deceives those who love not the truth, by virtue of the "lying wonders" which he effects (vss. 9, 10). Bloomfield calls these "pretended miracles" (p. 345). These "wonders" are not in the category with Christ's miracles. Lenski has well commented: "So many are ready to attribute real miracles to Satan and to his agents; the Scriptures never do" (1961, p. 426). In identifying the man of sin, one must thus look for a post-apostolic movement which claims to prove its authenticity by miracles.

(g) The early stages of this ecclesiastical apostasy were "already at work" in the first-century church (v. 7). The Greek term (*energeitai*, a present tense, middle voice form) suggests that this movement was currently working itself towards a greater goal. The child, later to become a man, was growing in Paul's day. The error was "already operative" (Lenski, 1961 p. 417), but not yet "revealed" (v. 6). This is a crucial point.

(h) In Paul's day there was some influence that "restrained" the budding man of sin. This was some sort of abstract force, as evidenced by the neuter form *to katechon*, "the restraining thing" (v. 6). And yet, this force was strongly associated with a person or persons as suggested by the masculine, "he who restrains" (v. 7). Likely the significance of this is that of a broad power, operating under individuals rulers. Unlike the man of sin, whose identity was later to be revealed, the early saints knew personally of this restraining force. "You know" (*oidate* - "to know from observation," Vine, p. 444). This indicates that the restraining force was an antique power, not a modern one.

(i) The restraining force eventually would "be taken out of the way," or, more correctly, "be gone." And so, the man of sin, in "his own season" would be clearly revealed (vss. 6, 7). Ellicott says that it is a season "appointed and ordained by God" (p. 121). One recalls that the "little horn" of Daniel's fourth beast only rose to prominence after three horns were plucked up to make room for it. Too, the earth-beast of John's vision came into full power after the sea-beast had received a death-stroke, but was healed. And so here, the restraining power will give way to the horrible revelation of the man of sin.

(j) The man of sin, though having roots in the world of ancient Christianity (v. 6), would nevertheless endure, in some form or another, until the end of time, i.e., until the second coming of Christ, at which time he will be destroyed by the Lord's word of judgment (vs. 8; cf. Rev. 19:15). In view of this, the man of sin cannot be some persecuting enemy that faded into oblivion centuries ago.

Theories Regarding the Man of Sin

Having surveyed the major elements that characterize the man of sin, we are now prepared to look at some of the current theories advanced in an effort to identify this sinister being.

Pagan Mythology

Liberal theologians contend that the notion of a man of sin reflects a belief in ancient, pagan mythology – endorsed by early Christians – which was incorporated into Paul's letter. This view rejects the conviction that the Scriptures are inspired of God; the concept is thus totally inconsistent with biblical claims, and proofs, regarding the inspiration of the apostolic documents.

Satan Himself

Some have argued that the man of sin is Satan himself. This view cannot be correct. Satan was not a part of "the falling away" (v. 3), and this "lawless one" is said to come "according to the working of Satan" (v. 9), which obviously distinguishes him from Satan personally.

Principle of Evil

Some allege that no specific power or person/persons are in view. Rather, the apostle has merely personified a principle, or idea of evil, which may appear in various forms in different historical periods as an opponent of truth. It may be manifest as

Islam, Fascism, Communism, etc. This concept does not fit the specific descriptives in this chapter. The text tells of a particular movement, "the falling away" (v. 3). How does that refer to Communism, etc.? Also, there are too many *personal* references to dismiss it as mere personification. Finally, it is "*the* man of sin," the article pointing to a definite influence, rather than a generic one.

Judaism

Radical Preterists (those who contend that all Bible prophecy, including the second coming of Christ, was fulfilled in the destruction of Jerusalem) argue that the man of sin was the "hardened, militant Jews (Zealots in particular)" (King, p. 318). This theory would thus see the man of sin (Judaism) destroyed by the coming of the Lord in the destruction of Jerusalem by the Romans in A.D. 70. The concept is totally false. Judaism was not a part of "the falling away" (v. 3). Moreover, Paul's prophecy of the second coming (the *parousia* – vs. 8) was not fulfilled in A.D. 70, as evidenced by the fact that Christians were not "gathered together" unto the Lord in connection with Jerusalem's fall (cf. 1 Thes. 4:14ff).

A Roman Ruler

A popular idea has it that the man of sin is a Roman ruler – perhaps Nero Caesar. Again, this concept does not fit the facts. No Caesar "fell away" from the faith (v. 3). Additionally, the Roman rulers have long lain in the dust of antiquity. As Raymond Kelcy observed: "Paul contemplates the man of lawlessness being in existence and waging opposition at the time the Lord returns; the Roman empire has long ago ceased to be" (p. 161).

The Future Antichrist

Millennialists (and some others) contend that the man of sin "is an individual embodying anti-God power who is still to arise before the future day of the Lord" (Mare, p. 1073). Hal Lindsey calls this hostile person "the Future Fuehrer," and he spends an entire chapter (Chapter 9) attempting to prove that "dramatic elements which are occurring in the world today are setting the stage for this magnetic, diabolical Future Fuehrer to make his entrance" (p. 102).

But Paul stated that the "mystery of iniquity," characteristic of the man of sin, was "already at work" (v. 7) in the first century. This clearly eliminates any person of the modern era. Newton's comment is appropriate: "As this evil began in the apostles' days, and was to continue in the world till the second coming of Christ in power and great glory: it necessarily follows, that it was to be carried on not by one man, but by a succession of men in several ages" (p. 453).

Identifying the Man of Sin

We believe that the best evidence indicates that the man of sin represents the *papal dynasty of the apostate church of Rome*. Barnes says: "Most Protestant commentators have referred it to the great apostasy under the Papacy ..." (1955, p. 80). Let us revisit the ten points of identification discussed earlier.

The Apostasy

The Roman Catholic system, with its autocratic papal dynasty, did not suddenly appear in a given year of history. Rather, it was the result of a gradual departure from the original faith. Paul declared: "The Spirit speaks expressly, that in later times some shall fall away from the faith ..." (1 Tim. 4:1). He details some of the traits of this movement, e.g., forbidding to marry, commanding to abstain from meats, etc. (1-4).

The many corruptions of the divine economy – changes in the plan of redemption (e.g., sprinkling, infant baptism, etc.), alteration of worship (e.g., the mass, the veneration of Mary, etc.) were progressively implemented. Catholicism evolved as a defection from the original faith. This history has been graphically detailed in John F. Rowe's classic volume, **The History of Apostasies** (1958, Rosemead, CA: Old Paths Publishing Co.).

Not Revealed in the First Century

The apostasy was just a budding phenomenon in the apostolic age. Consequently it was not fully "revealed" (v. 3) until centuries later.

Lawless

The Romish movement has exhibited a disposition of lawlessness throughout its sordid history. Could any citation better illustrate the spirit of lawlessness than this declaration regarding the papacy? "The pope doeth whatsoever he listeth [wills], even things unlawful, and is more than God" (quoted by Newton, p. 456). Attwater, a Catholic writer, has shown that, according to Roman Catholicism, "Tradition," i.e., the voice of the church, is superior to the Scriptures (pp. 41, 42). That is the very essence of lawlessness.

God-Opposing

The papacy opposes God. Surely anyone who claims to be "more than God" cannot be otherwise described than as an enemy of the Almighty.

Ecclesiastical Usurper of Divine Status

The papal rulers, as it were, "sit in the temple of God," i.e., the church; it is an *ecclesiastical* force. The pope claims that whereas Christ is the head of the church in heaven, the papacy is the head of the church on earth. Yet Jesus affirmed that he had "all authority ... in heaven and on earth" (Mt. 28:18). Paul stated that Christ is "*the* head [singular] of the body, the church" (Col. 1:18). Jesus does not share "headship" with the pope.

The papacy usurps the place of God by: (a) Making claims that belong only to deity – "Our Lord God the pope; another God upon the earth, king of kings, and lord of lords" (Newton, p. 456). (b) Accepting adoration not proper for a man. Men bow before the papal dignitary, kiss his feet, ring, etc. Contrast the disposition of Peter when Cornelius bowed before him (Acts 10:25, 26). (c) Presuming to act for God in matters pertaining exclusively to deity, e.g., offering forgiveness of sins. For example, in Catholic doctrine, "absolution" is a "judicial act whereby a priest remits the sins of a penitent who has contrition, has made confession and promises satisfaction" (Attwater, p. 3). The papal system lawlessly attempts to act for God.

Claim of Miracles

The whole history of Catholicism is checkered with the claims of "miracles." Conway, a Catholic apologist, states that God "has allowed His saints to work miracles to prove their divine commission to speak in His name, and to give the world a clear proof of their eminent sanctity. The Church always requires four, or in some instances six, miracles before she proceeds to beatify or canonize a saint" (p. 44).

Early Stages at Work in Paul's Day

Newton says: "The seeds of popery were sown in the apostle's time" (p. 457). Idolatry had invaded the church (1 Cor. 10:14), even in the worship of angels (Col. 2:18). Handling the word of God deceitfully (2 Cor. 4:2) had begun; strife and division were affecting the church (1 Cor. 3:3). Gospel truth was sacrificed for the sake of money (cf. 1 Tim. 6:5; Tit. 1:11) – compare the practice of "simony," i.e., the purchase of church offices, in Catholicism. Distinctions were made regarding meats (1 Cor. 8:8), and human traditions were creeping into the church (Col. 2:23). Certain men were beginning to exert preeminence and to flex their ecclesiastical muscles (3 Jn. 9, 10). Out of these attitudes and actions, the papacy finally was born.

Initially Restrained by Pagan Rome

If the man of sin is the papal dynasty, what was the force or person that "restrained" the initial revelation of this corrupt ecclesiastical system? McClintock and Strong, citing numerous sources from the early "church fathers" (e.g., Tertullian, Chrysostom, Hippolytus, Jerome, etc.), said that the patristic writers "generally consider" the restraining force to be "the Roman empire" (I p. 255). It is a matter of history that when imperial Rome fell in A.D. 476, great power was shifted into the hands of church clerics. If the restraining force was the Roman empire, and that force was removed in the 5th century A.D., does it not seem strange that the man of sin [Lindsey's "Fuehrer"] has not yet been made manifest – if the dispensational scheme of things is true?

Flourished After Fall of Rome

After imperial Rome fell, the apostate church of the day accelerated in its power. As mentioned earlier, great political authority was gained. Crowns were removed and bestowed at the behest of papal rulers. For example, in the 11th century of the Christian era, Emperor Henry IV sought to depose Pope Gregory VII (known as Hildebrand). In retaliation, Gregory excommunicated the emperor, and absolved all subjects from allegiance to him. Henry was powerless under the papal ban. In January, 1077, the emperor went to Canossa in northern Italy to beg the pope's forgiveness. He was forced to stand barefoot in the snow for three days, awaiting an audience with the pontiff (Hurlbut, 1954a, p. 111).

Other examples of the growing power of papal authority are numerous. "In Germany Emperor Frederick lay down on the floor and allowed Pope Alexander to stand on his neck. On another occasion, Pope Celestine III crowned Henry VI of England with the usual colorful ceremonies. As the English king knelt in front of him, after having had the crown of the British Empire placed upon his head, the pope reached forward with his foot and kicked the crown from the monarch's brow. At another time, Pope Alexander rode horseback down the streets of Rome. Walking along on either side of his horse, and leading the animal by the bridle, went Louis, King of France, and Henry, King of England" (Wilder, p. 103).

To Continue Until Christ's Return

The apostate church, an evolution from truth to error, clearly had its genesis in the first century; and yet, this movement continues to this day, and, according to Paul's prophecy, will abide, in one form or another, until the coming of Christ. "The apostasy" is the only system which fits the demands of this passage. It is both ancient and modern, something that cannot be said for a Caesar, the Jewish Zealots, or a modern Antichrist.

It is, of course, in vogue these days to ridicule this view of "the man of sin" as viewed in 2 Thessalonians, chapter 2. In reponse, one could hardly do better than to quote Coffman:

"[T]he identification of the papacy and its religious apparatus with Paul's words in 2 Thessalonians 2:3-10 was the prevailing view for more than a thousand years, a view supported by the writings and interpretations of many of the most brilliant men who ever lived on earth; and, on that account, there is no way for this writer to accept the sneers and snickers with which this interpretation is greeted by many modern commentators, as being an effective refutation of the arguments upholding it" (1986, p. 104).

In conclusion, we emphasize again, the "little horn" of Daniel 7, Paul's "man of sin," and "the beast" of the book of Revelation have much in common. These three images seem to reveal, in concert, one of the most vicious persecutors the church of God has ever known.

APPENDIX III

THE TIME IS "AT HAND"

There are those who contend that the whole of the book of Revelation, or a substantial portion thereof, was completely fulfilled – either within the first century, or very shortly thereafter. The advocates of realized eschatology (e.g., Max King and those influenced by him) are of this persuasion, as are others of the Preterist philosophy. Foy E. Wallace, Jr. argued that the Apocalypse was mostly fulfilled by A.D. 70. There are several vocabulary terms in Revelation which Preterists feel establish this point.

In the salutation of this book, John mentions the "things which must shortly [*en tachei*] come to pass" (1:1; 22:6). Subsequently, the text says: "for the time is at hand [*engus*]" (1:3; 22:10). There are also the claims of Christ: "I come quickly [*tachu*]" (2:16; 3:11; 22:7, 12, 20). All of these terms and phrases are supposed to be indicators that the book was to be fulfilled imminently. McGuiggan attempts to press this matter in proof of his contention that the entire book of Revelation was fulfilled in the church's victory over the ancient Roman empire (p. 13).

The fallacy in these views is that they fail to take into consideration that "time," within the context of prophecy, becomes extremely *relative*. There are numerous examples of this sort of chronological flexibility in the Scriptures – both in the Old Testament and in the New Testament. Really, there is no excuse for the serious Bible student not being aware of this idiomatic usage.

Shortly Come to Pass

Consider, for instance, the phrase, *en tachei*, rendered "shortly" in 1:1. The term can be used in different ways. Inspiration may be suggesting that the events described in this document would *begin* to unfold in the near future. Regarding "shortly," Jones observes: "This does not mean that everything revealed is to have immediate fulfillment. But all the things revealed are to begin having fulfillment shortly, and that process of fulfillment may go on for centuries" (p. 4).

On the other hand, *en tachei* can suggest the idea of speed, and thus *certainty*. Leon Morris says that "in the prophetic prospective the future is sometimes foreshortened. In other words the word [*en tachei*] may refer primarily to the certainty of the events in question" (p. 45). Another scholar observes: "By saying that events are to happen quickly John means that God will take an immediate hand in the events happening among the churches. He does not mean that everything envisioned will happen immediately ..." (Roberts, p. 28). As William Lee comments, this is time as "computed by God; not that the events are close at hand" (p. 497). This is the very point being made by the apostle Peter in his discussion of the Lord's coming and the end of the world (2 Pet. 3:8).

The same expression is found in Luke 18:8, where the Lord indicated that God will ultimately avenge his elect, and do so "speedily [*en tachei*]" (cf. Rev. 6:10, 11). He then asks: "Nevertheless, when the Son of man comes, shall he find faith on the earth?" The avenging was to be associated with the return of the Lord. It is obvious, therefore, that Christ was not telling the disciples that righteous grievances would be remedied in the *near future*. He was alluding to the judgment day. Clearly, *en tachei* can be used in a sense other than that of chronological proximity.

Robert Mounce points out that this is a book of prophecy, and "in the prophetic outlook the end is always imminent. This perspective is common to the entire New Testament. Jesus taught that God would vindicate his elect without delay (Lk. 18:8), and Paul wrote to the Romans that God would soon crush Satan under their feet (Rom. 16:20)" (p. 65). Both verses use *en tachei*.

At Hand

Does the expression "at hand" (*engus*) demand chronological nearness? In prophetic contexts, it certainly does not. Consider the following usages of the term in the Septuagint.

Deuteronomy 28 contains an amazing series of prophecies that preview the impending history of the nation of Israel. The Hebrew people are promised prosperity if they hearken diligently to the voice of their God (1). But they are warned that curses will be visited upon them if they refuse to listen to the Lord's commands (15). Tragically, the Hebrew people wandered away from Jehovah, and Moses' predictions were fulfilled precisely.

In chapter 32, a song of Moses is recorded. Therein the great prophet describes Israel's folly and the fact that God would eventually judge them. In that connection, this statement is made: "For the day of their calamity is *at hand*. And the things that are to come upon them shall make haste" (35). This prophecy was not fulfilled for many centuries. The statement was, of course, from the perspective of time *as God sees it*. The parallelism suggested in the second sentence – "shall make haste" – hints that the writer is speaking of a speedy, certain judgment. Historical time really is not a factor at all. As Robert Jamieson noted: "Although this awful judgment was not to be inflicted till a distant futurity, yet, as viewed through the telescope of prophecy, it might be said to be 'at hand'" (Jamieson, et al., p. 706).

Or consider this usage of *engus* by the prophet Obadiah. After discussing the destruction of Edom, the inspired writer looked into the distant future and tells of a "day of Jehovah" upon which "all the nations" are called to judgment. This cannot be a mere local judgment, as some have argued. As Coffman correctly observes, it "has reference to the final moral reckoning by the entire posterity of Adam at the time of the Second Advent of Our Lord Jesus Christ and the eternal judgment of all men" (1981, p. 258). See also Laetsch, (pp. 203-205). But consider how Obadiah has described this event: "For the day of Jehovah is near [*engus* – LXX] upon all the nations ..." (15). This surely demonstrates that *engus*, rendered as "near," or "at hand," etc., can have a relative meaning in contexts dealing with prophecy.

Another prophet announces: "Hold thy peace at the presence of the Lord Jehovah; for the day of Jehovah is at hand [*engus* – LXX] ..." (Zeph. 1:7). Again, "The great day of Jehovah is near [*engus*], it is near and hasteth greatly, even the voice of the day of Jehovah ..." (Zeph. 1:14). Zephaniah was a prophet in the days of Josiah (640-609 B.C.). The main point of his message is the coming "day of Jehovah." He begins with the general proposition that the entire earthly creation will be devastated by the coming judgment (1:1, 2). Then, representative examples (Judah, Philistia, Moab, etc., – 1:4, 5; 2:4-12) are selected to illustrate the impending doom to come. The temporal judgments inflicted upon these nations were but a preview of that great Judgment that loomed nearby, prophetically speaking.

These prophecies can refer to none other than the final day of human history, heralded by the second coming of Christ. David Baker has shown that the prophecy goes far beyond that of a "national import, but is shown here to affect all nations." It "culminates in Christ's second coming, the final day ..." (p. 99).

In the New Testament, a similar situation obtains. James admonishes the early saints: "Be ye also patient; establish your hearts: for the coming of the Lord is at hand [*engizo* - from *engus*]" (Jas. 5:8). "At hand" does not have a chronological significance in this prophetic passage; that is evident for two reasons: (a) No one knew when the coming of the Lord would occur (Mt. 24:36). Thus James could not have been suggesting that it was literally near. (b) It has been almost 2,000 years since James made this statement. Obviously, therefore, it did not denote chronological proximity. As Guy N. Woods pointed out: "We must not overlook the fact also that with God, who inhabits eternity, matters may be 'at hand,' in his view, which are greatly distant in our human imperfect concept" (p. 278).

In view of these clear biblical precedents, one must avoid the unwarranted notion that the entire book of Revelation had a complete fulfillment not long after the conclusion of the apostolic era.

Clearly, the "at hand" things of the Apocalypse were not all accomplished within the shadow of the first century. A recognition of this fact would prevent such an egregious error as the notion that the day of judgment occurred at the time of Jerusalem's destruction (King, p. 255ff), or the unjustified concept that the judgment of Revelation 20:11ff is merely a prediction of the fall of Rome (McGuiggan, pp. 307-309).

APPENDIX IV

WHEN WAS THE BOOK OF REVELATION WRITTEN?

Traditionally, the book of Revelation has been dated near the end of the first century, around A.D. 96. Across the years, however, a few writers have advanced the Preterist view ("preterist" is from a Latin word meaning "that which is past"), contending that the Apocalypse was penned around A.D. 68 or 69, and thus the major thrust of the book is supposed to relate to the impending destruction of Jerusalem (A.D. 70). Most of the book, it is claimed, was fulfilled in that event. According to this concept, the major thrust of the book has little, if any, prophetic relevance for a post-A.D. 70 audience.

A few prominent names have been associated with this position (e.g., Moses Stuart, Phillip Schaff, and J.B. Lightfoot). George Salmon, whose widely-read volume, **Introduction to the New Testament** was a death-blow to certain critical theories, once entertained the preterist concept, but eventually he abandoned it (p. 242).

Within churches of Christ, Foy E. Wallace, Jr. contended for this position. For a while the preterist theory enjoyed a modest level of respectability among some scholars, but, as James Orr observed, more recent criticism has reverted to the traditional date of approximately A.D. 96 (IV, p. 2584).

This writer believes that the evidence for the later date is extremely strong. And, in view of some of the bizarre theories that have surfaced in the Lord's church in recent times (e.g., the "radical preterism" of Max R. King) – that are dependent upon a pre-A.D. 70 dating scheme – we offer the following evidence for a later chronology of the book.

External Evidence

The external evidence for the late dating of Revelation is of the highest quality.

(1) Irenaeus (c. A.D. 180), a student of the renowned Polycarp (who was a disciple of the apostle John), declared that the Apocalyptic vision "was seen not very long ago, almost in our own generation, at the close of the reign of Domitian" (**Against Heresies**, V.30). The testimony of Irenaeus, not far removed from the apostolic age, is first-rate, and he places the book near the end of Domitian's reign. Domitian died in A.D. 96. Irenaeus seems to be unaware of any other view of the book's date.

(2) Clement of Alexandria (c. A.D. 155-215) says that John returned from the isle of Patmos "after the tyrant was dead," (**Who Is The Rich Man?** 42). Eusebius, known as the "father of church history," (c. A.D. 324) identifies the "tyrant" as Domitian (**Ecclesiastical History**, III.23). Even Moses Stuart (1780-1852), America's most prominent preterist in his day, admitted that the "tyrant here meant is probably Domitian." Within this narrative Clement further speaks of John as an "old man." If Revelation was written prior to A.D. 70, it would scarcely seem appropriate to refer to John, who would then be but in his early sixties, as an "old man." Particularly is this the case since Timothy, in his thirties, was still called a "youth" (1 Tim. 4:12; cf. Conybeare & Howson, p. 830). It has been objected, though, that Clement represents the apostle as running, and that such could hardly have been true of a man near ninety. But Clement specifically says that John ran, being "forgetful of his age."

(3) Victorinus (late 3rd C.), author of the earliest commen-

tary on the book of Revelation, wrote: "When John said these things, he was in the island of Patmos, condemned to the mines by Caesar Domitian. There he saw the Apocalypse; and when at length grown old, he thought that he should receive his release by suffering; but Domitian being killed, he was liberated" (**Commentary on the Revelation**, 10:11).

(4) Jerome (A.D. 340-420) said, "In the fourteenth then after Nero, Domitian having raised up a second persecution, he [John] was banished to the island of Patmos, and wrote the Apocalypse ..." (**Lives of Illustrious Men**, 9).

(5) To all of this may be added the comment of Eusebius, who contends that the historical tradition of his time (c. A.D. 324) placed the writing of the Apocalypse at the close of Domitian's reign (**Eccl. Hist.**, III.18).

McClintock and Strong, in contending for the later date, declare that "there is no mention in any writer of the first three centuries of any other time or place." (VIII, p. 1064). Upon the basis of external evidence therefore, there is little contest between the earlier and later dates.

On the matter of external support, some of the older writers argued for an early date on the basis of a superscription in the Peshitta Syriac version (thought to date from the 2nd C.) which asserted John was banished to Patmos in Nero's reign. It is now known that the Peshitta is but a 5th century revision of the Old Syriac, which did not even contain the book of Revelation (Robertson, 1925, p. 114).

Internal Evidence

The evidence within the book of Revelation also suggests a late date, as the following observations reveal.

(1) The spiritual conditions of the churches mentioned in

chapters 2 and 3 seem to harmonize better with the late date. "The church in Ephesus, for instance, was not founded by Paul until the latter part of Claudian's reign: and when he wrote to them from Rome, A.D. 61, instead of reproving them for any want of love, he commends their love and faith. (Eph. 1:15)" (Horne, II, p. 382). Yet when Revelation was written, in spite of the fact that the Ephesians had been patient for a while (2:2), they also had left their first love (2:4). This would appear to require a greater lapse of time than a mere seven or eight years, as the earlier date would demand.

(2) The book was penned while John was banished to Patmos (1:9). It is well-known that Domitian had a fondness for this type of persecution. (Eusebius, III.18). Besides, it hardly appears reasonable that Nero, who is reported to have beheaded Paul and crucified Peter (Eusebius, II. 25), would have been content merely to banish their co-apostle to isolation.

(3) The church at Laodicea is represented as existing under conditions of great wealth. "Thou sayest, I am rich, and have gotten riches, and have need of nothing" (3:17). In A.D. 60, however, Laodicea had been almost entirely destroyed by an earthquake. It seems likely that it would have required more than a brief eight or nine years to once again rise to the description conveyed in Revelation.

(4) The doctrinal departures described in Revelation appear to fit better the later dating. For example, the Nicolaitans (see 2:6, 15) were a robust sect at the time of John's writing, whereas they had only been hinted at in very general terms in 2 Peter and Jude, which were written possibly around A.D. 65-66.

(5) Persecution for those professing the Christian faith is evident in the letters to the churches of Asia Minor (chapters 2 & 3). For instance, Antipas had been killed in Pergamum (2:13).

It is generally agreed among scholars, though, that "Nero's persecution seems to have been confined to Rome and was not for religious reasons" (Harrison, p. 446).

Arguments for the Early Date Answered

In the absence of external evidence in support of the early dating of Revelation, preterists generally rely on what they perceive to be internal support for their view. Let us consider a few of their arguments.

The *most popular argument* for the early date suggests that John's Gospel is characterized by a much smoother style of Greek than is the Apocalypse. It is supposed, therefore, that the latter must have been written many years prior to the Gospel, when the apostle was not so experienced in the employment of literary Greek. To this assertion it may be replied:

(1) "Archaeological discoveries and literary studies have recently demonstrated that along with Aramaic and Hebrew, Greek was commonly spoken among first century Palestinians. Thus John must have known and used Greek since his youth." (Gundry, p. 365).

(2) B.B. Warfield contended that "the Apocalypse betrays no lack of knowledge of, or command over, Greek syntax or vocabulary: the difference lies, rather, in the manner in which a language well in hand is used, in style, properly so called; and the solution of it must turn on psychological, and not chronological, considerations." (Schaff, 1894, III p. 2036).

(3) R.H. Charles, author of the commentary on Revelation in the **International Critical Commentary** series, and probably the greatest expert ever on apocalyptic literature, regarded the so-called "bad grammar" as *deliberate*, for purposes of emphasis, as well as the use of Old Testament passages in Hebraic

style. Charles did not consider John's grammar to be the result of ignorance or blundering. (Vol. I, pp. cxvii-clix). Westcott and Hort's **Greek New Testament** cites more than 500 references and allusions to the Old Testament in the 404 verses of the book of Revelation.

(4) McClintock and Strong point out: "It may be admitted that the Revelation has many surprising grammatical peculiarities. But much of this is accounted for by the fact that it was probably written down, as it was seen, 'in the Spirit,' while the ideas, in all their novelty and vastness, filled the apostle's mind, and rendered him less capable of attending to forms of speech. His Gospel and Epistles, on the other hand, were composed equally under divine influence, but an influence of a gentler, more ordinary kind, with much care, after long deliberation, after frequent recollection and recital of the facts, and deep pondering of the doctrinal truths which they involve" (VIII, p.1064.)

A *second argument* advanced in favor of the early date is this. It is claimed that Revelation must have been penned prior to A.D. 70, because it contains no allusion to the destruction of Jerusalem. Rather, it is alleged, it represents both the city and the temple as still standing.

But, if John wrote this work near A.D. 96, there would be little need to emphasize the destruction of Jerusalem that occurred *almost a third of a century earlier,* since the lessons of that catastrophe would have been well learned in the preceding decades. Besides, some scholars see a figurative reference to Jerusalem's destruction in 11:8, where the city is symbolically depicted as "Sodom," i.e., a city destroyed by divine judgment, and "Egypt," – the place where the Lord was crucified.

Moreover, the contention that the literal city and temple were still standing ignores the express symbolic nature of the narrative.

George Salmon says of Revelation 11 that it is "difficult to understand how anyone could have imagined that the vision represents the temple as still standing. For the whole scene is laid in heaven, and the temple that is measured is the heavenly temple. (11:19; 15:5). We have only to compare this vision with the parallel vision of a measuring-reed seen by Ezekiel (ch. 40), in which the prophet is commanded to measure – surely not the city which it is stated had been demolished fourteen years previously, but the city of the future seen by the prophet in vision" (p. 238).

A *third argument* for an early date of the Apocalypse is posed by asserting that the enigmatical number, 666 (13:18), is a reference to Nero (who died in A.D. 68). This is a real stretch. This mysterious number finds a connection with "Nero" only if one: (a) adds the title "Caesar" to Nero's name; (b) computes the title-name on the basis of the *Hebrew* language (though Revelation was written in *Greek*); and, (c) alters the Hebrew spelling of "Caesar" by dropping the letter *yodh*. All of this reveals a desperate attempt to find Nero in the passage.

Additionally, as Leon Morris pointed out, Irenaeus discussed a number of views as to what 666 might symbolize, yet he did not include Nero anywhere on his list, let alone regard this as a likely conjecture (p. 38). Furthermore, noted critic Theodor Zahn contended that the name "Nero" was never even set forth as a possibility for 666 until suggested by Fritzsche in the year 1831 (p. 447).

In view of the foregoing data – external and internal – the date of the book of Revelation at around A.D. 96 best fits all of the known facts.

APPENDIX V

JESUS CHRIST: THE FIRST AND THE LAST

The book of Revelation opens with John the apostle exiled to the island of Patmos. He "was in the Spirit on the Lord's day" when he heard a loud voice behind him. As he turned to see who had spoken, he beheld the Lord Jesus – upon whose blessed countenance his eyes had not rested in more than sixty years.

The apostle was terrified and fell toward the Lord's feet. Christ sought to comfort him, admonishing: "Stop being afraid (so the emphasis in the Greek text), I am the first and the last, and the living one; I was dead, and behold, I am alive forever and ever, and I have the keys of death and Hades" (1:17-18).

In this discussion, we wish to focus special attention upon the phrase, "the first and the last." It implies a number of important things.

Jesus Christ: Eternal

Note that the phrase is expanded later in the book. As Revelation is concluded, the Lord affirms: "I am the Alpha and the Omega, the first and the last, the beginning and the end" (22:13; cf. 21:6). This is a clear declaration of the eternal nature of Christ, hence, his deity.

Consider that the expression "Alpha and Omega" is applied to the Father in 1:8. This passage and numerous others demonstrate that the "Jehovah's Witnesses" are seriously in error when they deny that the personal Word (Jn. 1:1, 14) is eternal in his existence, and contend that he was the first of God's created beings. The Bible makes it abundantly clear that there never was a time when the Second Person in the Godhead did not exist (cf. Mic. 5:2; Isa. 9:6; Jn. 1:1-3; 8:58).

For a more complete discussion of this matter, see our booklet, **Jehovah's Witnesses and the Doctrine of the Deity of Christ**.

Jesus Christ: Unique

The expressions "the first and the last" and "the Living one" also suggest the uniqueness of Christ. He stands in bold relief to the non-gods of pagan idolatry.

An Old Testament prophet, speaking for the Lord, declared: "... I am the first, and I am the last; and besides me there is no god" (Isa. 44:6). Paul commended the saints at Thessalonica in that they "turned unto God from idols, to serve a living and true God" (1 Thes. 1:9).

The Christian religion stands in a class by itself with reference to its concept of God, as manifested in the Father, the Son, and the Holy Spirit.

Jesus Christ: Sovereign Creator

Christ is also "the first and the last" with reference to the material universe. The preincarnate Lord was present at the creation event, and he was an active agent in the process.

The plural form *elohim* (God) in Genesis 1:1 hints of this (Stone, p. 11), and that thought is expanded in 1:26. "Let us make man in our image, after our likeness ..." (cf. 11:7; Isa. 6:8). An apostle plainly says that "[a]ll things were made through him; and without him was not anything made that was made" (Jn. 1:3; cf. 1 Cor. 8:6; Col. 1:16; Heb. 1:2).

Elsewhere in the book of Revelation, Jesus is designated as

"the beginning of the creation of God" (3:14). This does not suggest, as the Watchtower Witnesses propose, that Jesus was the first of God's created ones; rather, it stresses his role as Creator. The Greek word for "beginning" is *arche*, which, in this context indicates "that by which anything begins to be, the origin, active cause" (Thayer, 77). A.T. Robertson called *arche* "the originating source of the creation" (1933, VI, 321).

On the other hand, it is also true that Jesus will bring the material universe to a conclusion at the time of his return. Note Paul's declaration: "Then comes the end, when he [Christ] shall deliver up the kingdom to God, even the Father; when he shall have abolished all rule and all authority and power. For he must reign, till he hath put all his enemies under his feet. The last enemy that shall be abolished is death" (1 Cor. 15:24-26).

In Second Peter, chapter 3, there is a discussion of Christ's "coming" to render judgment (cf. 4). On that "day of the Lord" the "heavens shall pass away with a great noise, and the elements shall be dissolved with fervent heat, and the earth and the works that are therein shall be burned up" (10). The notion that this chapter refers merely to the destruction of Jerusalem is utterly without merit (see Jackson 1990a, 78-79).

Jesus Christ: Savior

Christ is "the first and the last" with reference to the gospel system as well. The writer of Hebrews characterizes the Lord as "the author" (*archegos* - the beginner, the leader) and "the finisher" (*teleiotes* - one who brings to completion) of "the faith" (12:2).

The expression "the faith" (the article is in the Greek text) represents the sum total of the gospel plan of redemption. This sacred operation needs no modification from sinful men. Let those who would add to, delete from, or alter the divine scheme in any way desist from such.

We are complete "in Christ" (Col. 2:10). We have no need for the mediation of angels or "saints," and no refinement from councils or popes is required. Everything to sustain us is in the gospel package. Thanks be to God for his unspeakable gift (2 Cor. 9:15), who is the first and the last.

APPENDIX VI

MARGINAL NOTES FROM THE BOOK OF REVELATION

Chapter 1

1:1

The final book of the New Testament commences with a declaration that it involves the "revelation of Jesus Christ." Actually it is a revelation *from* Christ, and it is a revelation *about* the Lord. He is the source of the instruction and the theme involves his ultimate victory over evil.

The message was to be sent and signified by an angel to the apostle John. Of special interest is the term "signified." The Greek word is *semaino*, and it is related to the root form *sema*, "a sign," hence it suggests that the message is to be conveyed by a series of signs. Simply speaking, the book is to be characterized by symbols. Underline "signified" and marginally note: *A book of symbols; cf. John 21:19.*

Revelation is a book of prophecy (v. 3). Accordingly, due to the fact that inspiration describes the events that are to unfold as "shortly" coming to pass, some have erroneously concluded that the entire book was fulfilled within a brief time following John's reception of the message. But that conclusion is not necessary. The word rendered "shortly" can denote that which happens with quickness (cf. Luke 18:8 - "speedily"). It may therefore hint of the decisiveness with which the Lord will deal with his foes.

If the term does have a chronological significance in this context, it could simply suggest that the events depicted may commence to unfold in the not-distant future. Underscore "shortly" and make notations reflecting these points.

1:3

Within the opening salutation, a blessing is pronounced on those who hear the words of this prophecy and "keep" the things that are written. Underline the term "keep." It contains a crucial implication. While this book contains some mysterious symbols, it obviously can be comprehended to a significant degree. One cannot *keep* what he cannot understand. But this narrative contains obligations to be kept. So one must study and seek to understand the document. Underline "keep" and note: *Understand and obey.*

Observe that verse 3 takes the form of a beatitude. "Blessed is he ..." This is the first of seven "blessed" statements within the book (1:3; 14:13; 16:15; 19:9; 20:6; 22:7, 14). Underscore "blessed," and list these references in your margin beside verse 3.

1:4

The Revelation was primarily addressed to the "seven churches of Asia." There were other congregations in Asia (i.e., Troas - Acts 20:5; Colossae - Col. 1:2; Hierapolis - Col. 4:13). These seven were probably simply representative of the needs of God's people at large. Circle "seven" and note: *Representative churches.*

Note there is a salutation from him who is, was, and is to come, from the seven Spirits before the throne, and from Christ. Underline the expression "seven Spirits," and marginally note that this is likely an allusion to the Holy Spirit – the numeral "seven" suggesting the completeness of his work (cf. 3:1; 4:5; 5:6).

1:5

Three things are said regarding Christ in this verse. He is the "faithful witness" – faithful in life (1 Pet. 2:22) and faithful in teaching (John 14:6). He is also the "firstborn of the dead." Of all those raised from the dead (e.g., Lazarus), only the Lord remained alive (cf. v. 18; Rom. 6:9). Therefore, "firstborn" suggests preeminence (cf. Col. 1:18). Make a note to that effect.

Finally, Jesus is the "ruler of the kings of the earth." This designation would be quite meaningful to Christians who were being persecuted in a time when it appeared that earth's political dignitaries were in control of human affairs. This verse emphasizes the sovereignty of the Lord Jesus and is clear testimony of his deity. Make a brief marginal note to this effect.

1:9

John states that he is a "partaker" in the kingdom along with the Christians who constituted the seven congregations of Asia. This is positive proof that the "kingdom" was a present reality. This truth is in conflict with the premillennial theory that the Lord's kingdom will not be established until the time of the Second Coming. Circle "partaker" and "kingdom" and connect the two with a line. In your margin, record: *Kingdom a present reality.* One might also reference Colossians 1:13 where the apostle Paul argues that Christians have been "translated" (past tense) into Christ's kingdom.

Additionally, one might wish to note some geographical information regarding the island of Patmos. It is located about 70 miles southwest of Ephesus. It is about 20 miles in circumference and covers an area of about 50 square miles.

1:13

On a lonely Lord's day (v. 10), John saw a remarkable vision of the risen Son of God. The description given in verse 13 is reminiscent of the priestly adornment of Old Testament literature (cf. Ex. 28:4). The vision is, therefore, likely to suggest the priestly function of the Lord. Bracket this verse and note: *Priestly apparel; see Exodus 28:4.*

This being the case, it is interesting to observe that in the initial chapter of Revelation, all three offices of Christ are portrayed. He is a prophet (vv. 1, 3); a king (v. 5); and a priest (v. 13). Somewhere in the margin, call attention to this three-fold function of the Savior.

1:18

When Christ spoke to John in this unique interview on Patmos, he informed the apostle that he (Christ) possessed the "keys of death and of Hades." The term "keys" is a figure of speech suggesting that one possesses the authority to open (cf. Matt. 16:19).

Observe also that the word "keys" is plural, indicating that there is a distinction between "death," the state of the body, and "Hades," the abode of the soul (Acts 2:27). This is a powerful argument demonstrating that man is more than merely a body of flesh. He possesses a soul as well. Make notations to this effect in your margin.

In connection with this point, consider also the references to death and Hades in chapter 20:13-14.

Chapter 2

2:1

Inspiration states that Christ walked in the midst of the seven golden candlesticks. What is the significance of such a statement? Earlier, the apostle informs us that the "seven golden candlesticks" are actually representations of the seven congregations of Asia (1:20). Thus, when it is affirmed that Jesus walks (a continuous action form) among the congregations, it is an indication that he is constantly in association with his churches. What a word of comfort this was to those ancient saints who were so distressed with persecution! Is the Lord nearby? Yes, indeed! Underline "walketh in the midst" and note: *The abiding presence of Christ among his churches; see 1:20.*

2:2

There are those who utterly abhor the concept of church discipline. However, Jesus *commended* the church in Ephesus because they put to the test certain men who claimed to be apostles but were not. The faithful portion of the church found them false. The implication is that those false apostles were rejected by the church. Mark this expression and marginally note: *Church discipline commended.*

2:5

Can a Christian fall from grace? Many religionists allege that he cannot. But this passage demonstrates otherwise.

The Lord informed the Ephesian Christians that some had left their first love, i.e., the quality of love they had when they first embraced the truth. He admonished them to remember whence they had "fallen" (Gal. 5:4). Jesus further warned that if they did not repent, he would move their "candlestick" from its place. Since the candlestick was the church itself (1:20), they were in danger of losing their identity as a church of Christ. Underscore "fallen," and marginally comment: *A Christian can fall; see Gal. 5:4.*

Additionally, observe the Lord's threat. If these brothers do not repent, he will "come" in judgment upon them. It is important to understand that not every instance in Scripture alluding to the Lord's "coming" is a reference to his Second Coming at the end of the world. This is the common error of those who subscribe to the dogma of realized eschatology – the notion that in A.D. 70, with the destruction of Jerusalem, the Second Coming of Christ occurred.

This passage, along with others (cf. 2:16), reveals that there is a sense in which Jesus can "come" that is not synonymous with his ultimate coming on the Day of Judgment. Hence, underline "come" and in your margin note: *Not the Second Coming: cf. 2:16.*

2:10

Christ instructed the saints in Smyrna to be "faithful unto death, and I will give thee the crown of life." This admonition is not merely to remain faithful until the time of death. This passage clearly shows the real value of Christianity. It is a system which requires, if need be, the forfeiture of one's physical life. Circle the term "unto" and in your margin observe: *To the extent of – demonstrates the value of Christianity.*

2:11

One of the key words in the book of Revelation is "overcome." Each of the seven congregations of Asia is encouraged to overcome the tribulations which come against them (see 2:7, 12, 17, 26; 3:5, 12, 21).

To Smyrna, Christ says: "He that overcomes shall not be hurt of the second death." In Bible parlance, the term "death" always connotes a separation of some sort. In the present instance, the use of the expression "second death" implies a first death. The first death is physical death, at which point the spirit is separated from the body (Jas. 2:26). The second death is the final separation from God which occurs at the time of the Judgment Day. It is the same state as "hell." In chapter 20, the apostle writes: "And death and Hades were cast into the lake of fire. This is the second death, even the lake of fire" (Rev. 20:14). Underline "second death" in 2:11 and in your margin note: *Eternal punishment; see 20:14.*

2:17

Each of the seven churches is promised certain blessings if they "overcome" the difficulties that assault their faith. To the saints in Pergamum, one of those promises of victory was a "white stone."

Several explanations have been offered as the meaning of this mysterious expression. Perhaps one of the more plausible is that it refers to a court verdict of innocence. In ancient times, a jury would vote by casting stones into a container. If a black stone was deposited, the verdict was guilty; white signified acquittal. When Paul referred to his preconversion opposition to Christians, he said: "I gave my vote [*psephos* – stone] against them" (Acts 26:10). The symbol may thus suggest that even though the ancient Christians had been condemned in the court of world opinion, in Heaven's court they would be vindicated. Underline "white stone," and note: *Possible symbol of innocence; cf. Acts 26:10.*

2:20

In the church at Thyatira, there was a woman who was designated as "Jezebel" – probably a figure suggesting that she was as evil as her Old Testament namesake. One of "Jezebel's" sins was that she *taught* Christians to commit *fornication*. This passage illustrates the truth that not only is it folly to personally engage in immoral conduct, it is an egregious error to teach that which encourages sin in others. Since "fornication" is an umbrella term which includes many forms of sexual perversion, one may reflect upon the following. There are those who teach that: homosexuality is an acceptable alternate form of indulgence; unmarried couples may engage in sexual activity with impunity if they really love one another; new unions may be entered justifiably after divorces for non-biblical reasons (i.e., not for fornication – Matt. 19:9).

Anyone who endorses and encourages sexual sin by his or her false teaching is a modern "Jezebel." Underline "teacheth" and "fornication" and in your margin note: *Danger of teaching falsely regarding sexual conduct.*

Chapter 3

3:2

Christ is ever aware of what is transpiring within his congregations. He reminded the church in Sardis, "I know your works" (3:1). The Lord then informed this group of saints: "I have found no works of thine perfected before my God." There are those in the church who are ever commencing projects but never completing them. They are start-and-stop Christians. Jesus wants progressive, steadfast growth from his people. Bracket off this clause and marginally note: *steadfastness needed; see 1 Corinthians 15:58.*

3:5

We must constantly remind ourselves that the theme of the Apocalypse is *overcoming*. Great promises are made to those who overcome the opposition of Satan and his henchmen. First, those who overcome are promised white garments. The adjective "white" is common to Revelation. Of the 26 times the term is used in the New Testament, 16 are in the final book. Depending upon the context, the word can denote either purity or victory. Here, both ideas are likely combined. There is a connection between purity and victory. Underline "white," and in your margin record: *Purity, victory.*

Second, the promise is made that those who overcome will not be blotted out of the book of life. The implication is obvious. Those who *do not* overcome *will be* blotted out of the book of life. But one cannot be blotted out of the book who has not been recorded therein. It is therefore clear that this passage affords a warning that it is possible for a Christian to fall from the faith and finally lose his salvation. Note in your margin: *the dogma of the impossibility of apostasy is false.*

3:7

Christ is described as possessing the "key of David" so that when he opens, none can shut; and when he shuts, none can open. What is the significance of this statement? It has its background in the book of Isaiah. During the reign of Hezekiah an ambitious official in the king's administration, Shebna by name, was removed from his position. He was replaced by Eliakim, who was given the "key of the house of David" with absolute power to open and shut (Isa. 22:22). The expression signified the royal authority of his office. This language, employed here of Christ, is a clear affirmation of the Lord's regal authority (cf. Matt. 28:18). Underline the phrase "key of the house of David" and comment: *Royal authority. See Isaiah 22:15ff for background.*

3:12

Jesus had no word of censure for the church in Philadelphia. Among the promises proffered for this congregation's sustained fidelity, the Lord declared that the faithful would "go out thence no more." Some scholars, e.g., William Barclay (1957, p. 81), have observed that Philadelphia was a city constantly threatened by earthquakes. In A.D. 17, a quake had devastated the city. The inhabitants of this area were repeatedly having to evacuate the community. The expression "go out thence no more" may be an allusion to this circumstance. The flavor may be: "If you remain faithful to the truth, you will no more live in fear." You may wish to underline this phrase and marginally comment: *Possible allusion to area earthquakes; promise of fearless environment.*

3:14

In the opening line of the letter to the church in Laodicea, Jesus describes himself as "the beginning of the creation of God." The "Jehovah's Witnesses" cite this passage in an attempt to prove that the Lord was not an eternal being. It is the contention of the Watchtower advocates that Christ was the first thing that Jehovah God created. The allegation is patently false.

We must emphasize two points. First, the Greek term rendered "beginning" is *arche*. Language scholars are united in affirming that this very term means *originating cause* in the context under consideration (cf. Arndt & Gingrich, p. 111).

Second, since Jesus is characterized as both "the beginning" and "the end" later in this book (22:13), if one argues that "beginning" denotes the commencement of the Lord's existence, then "end" would seem to suggest the termination of his existence – a conclusion hardly accepted, even by the "Witnesses."

Circle "beginning," and marginally note: *Originating cause.*

3:16

It is a sad commentary on the people of the Laodicean church that the Son of God could not find a single trait in them to commend. He described them as being spiritually "lukewarm." They made the Lord sick and he, in a manner of speaking, threatened to vomit them out. What is lukewarmness that makes it so reprehensible in Jesus' sight? There are two passages which may shed light on this matter.

In his epistle to Titus, Paul describes some who are "abominable, and disobedient, and unto every good work reprobate" (1:16). Such people, one supposes, are spiritually "cold." On the other hand, Christ desires that his people be "zealous of good works" (Tit. 2:14). Such zeal would represent those who are "hot" in the Savior's service. The "lukewarm," it would appear, stand somewhere between these two extremes and are dangerous in their influence. In such a context, Sunday-morning-only saints come to mind. Underscore "lukewarm" and in the margin note: *See Titus 1:16; 2:14 for cold and hot examples.*

3:21

Christ promised that those who overcome will be able to sit down with him in his throne, just as he overcame and sat down with his Father in his throne. Notice the past tense form, "sat down." This passage makes premillennialists uncomfortable since they allege that Jesus will not be enthroned until the time of his Second Coming. But this affirmation is perfectly consistent with other New Testament references which picture the Lord as reigning in this present economy. Underline "sat down" and note the tense in your margin. Add this comment: *See also Acts 2:30-31; 1 Cor. 15:24-25. Premillennialism is false.*

Chapter 4

4:1

In Revelation 4, John saw a door into heaven standing open. (Such is the force of the original language construction.) This is an invitation for the apostle to look in. The language is similar to that of Ezekiel 1:1, where that Old Testament prophet received a similar vision preparatory to his revelations from the Lord. Underline "opened" and marginally note: *See Ezekiel 1:1.*

A voice spoke to John, inviting him to "come up" so that he might be shown the things that "must" come to pass hereafter. Mark that "must." It reveals the sovereignty of God. In your margin write: *God is in charge of history.*

4:2

As John beheld the splendid vision, he was "in the Spirit" (cf. 1:10), and he saw a heavenly throne, with God, the Father, sitting on it. The language is reminiscent of Old Testament imagery wherein Jehovah is shown to be in control over the nations of the world (Ps. 47:8). This would be important to the saints since, in their state of persecution, it would appear as if the political forces of the ancient world were in command. Underscore "sitting upon the throne" and note: *See Psalm 47:8. God has not lost control.*

4:3

It is impossible to know the precise form that God assumed as John viewed him upon the throne. He may have appeared human-like (cf. "hand" in 5:1), though the imagery is likely anthropomorphic (i.e., God symbolically depicted in human form). The Lord seems to have been bathed in brilliant light, perhaps the same suggestion as that conveyed in 1 Timothy 6:16. Bracket this verse and note that reference in your margin.

Observe also the allusion to the "rainbow" which was a symbol in Genesis of both *judgment and mercy* – a prevalent theme of this book: judgment upon God's enemies; mercy toward his people. Circle "rainbow" and comment: *Symbol of judgment and mercy.*

4:4

Sitting around the throne of God were twenty-four elders, clothed in white garments, with golden crowns on their heads. Who were these "elders"? They probably represent some sort of order of angels. Later they appear to be distinguished from those who are purchased with the Lamb's blood – contrast the "them" with "our" (Rev. 5:9-10) – which would seem to take them out of the human class. Mark "elders" and note: *Possibly angels; see Rev. 5:9-10.* Then circle those pronouns in verse 10.

Their "white" garments suggest *purity*. Their "crowns" hint that they are endowed with some kind of *authority*. Apparently there is an order of authority among angels (Jude 6). Make notes to this effect.

4:5

Lightnings, voices, and thunders are symbols of God's power and sovereignty. Note: *See Exodus 19:16ff; Ps. 18:12ff; 77:18.*

4:6-8

Near the throne of God were "four living creatures" (not "beasts" – KJV). Who were these living creatures? Some see them as another order of angels. They are clearly similar to the creatures depicted in the book of Ezekiel (Ezek. 1:10; 10:20). They combine the traits of several beings of earth's creation – lion, calf, eagle, man.

Some feel that the symbols may therefore represent animate nature, and so suggest that God is worthy of honor by his entire creation. This is a possible meaning, though the worship of the creatures seems to be later distinguished from that of "every created thing" (Rev. 5:11, 13). Clearly, the bottom line of the whole context is that God, because of his nature, is worthy of the praise of every created thing – in heaven and earth. Bracket these verses and note: *God is worthy of praise: cf. Psalm 18:3.*

4:8

This anthem of praise is similar to that uttered by the seraphim in Isaiah's throne room scene (Isa. 6:1ff). The triple form "Holy, holy, holy" stresses the absolutely sinless nature of the Creator. He is too pure to look upon sin in any sort of favorable way (Hab. 1:13). Block off this passage and comment: *Absolute purity of God.*

The verse actually delineates three characteristics of the Creator. He is *holy, all-powerful, and eternal.* Mark these points.

4:11

God is honored for his brilliant creative power. All things were created by him. This implies, of course, that the universe is neither eternal nor self-created, as asserted by the atheistic community. "God" is the only sufficient cause of the creation. Jot in your margin: *Creation neither eternal nor self-created.*

It is difficult to fathom the wickedness of those who attempt to explain the universe by means of evolutionary processes. The phrase "they *were* [imperfect tense – suggesting progressive activity], and *were created* [aorist tense – viewing the creation as an event]" seems to suggest that the entire potential creation passed before the mind of God, and then, by the power of the Almighty, there came the awesome events of Genesis 1.

Chapter 5

5:1-3

In the previous chapter the emphasis was upon God, the Father. Now, the Son will step to the forefront. In the "right hand" (a suggestion of *importance*) of God, John saw a scroll written on "both sides" (perhaps hinting of the *completeness* of the message). Underline "right hand" and "both sides" and enter these notes.

The book was sealed, however, with seven seals. No created being anywhere was "worthy" to open it. This implies that someone, *above* the creature-class would be needed to accomplish the task. Why? Because only *Deity* knows the future. Connect and underline "no one" and "was able," and marginally record: *A demand for Deity.*

5:4-5

When John contemplated the fact that the message of the scroll might remain concealed, he wept much. The Greek expression means to cry aloud, and in a sustained fashion. Make a note to that effect.

John was told to stop weeping because the Lion from the

tribe of Judah had overcome. The term "Lion" is probably a reference to the prophecy of Genesis 49:9. Circle the term and enter that reference. The allusion is to the royal authority of Christ.

The Lord is designated as "the Root of David." "Root" is generally viewed as a reference to the fact that Jesus was descended from David. However, a "root" is normally the source from which the plant springs (cf. 1 Tim. 6:10). Moreover, in Revelation 22:16, Christ is called both the "root" and "offspring," which would seem to suggest that "root" is to be distinguished from "offspring." Therefore, "root" likely asserts that Christ existed *before* Israel's great king, and that he was ultimately the *source* of the monarch (cf. John 8:58; Matt. 22:42-45). Circle "root" and marginally note: *Source (cf. 22:6); evidence of Jesus' deity.*

Finally, observe that the Lion "hath overcome." The past tense form declares the fact that Jesus has already won the victory. Everything else is just mopping up! What a thrilling declaration this must have been to those persecuted Christians!

5:6

John saw, in the midst of the throne, a Lamb. Jesus is referred to as a Lamb in eleven different chapters of this book (for a total of twenty-seven times). Clearly the reference is to the sacrificial work of Jesus (cf. John 1:29). Circle "Lamb," and note: *Offering of Jesus for sin; see John 1:29.*

The Lamb "had been slain." The perfect tense participle indicates that the effect of the Lamb's death lingered after the event itself. There was an on-going blessing as a result of Calvary. Jesus did not have to die for each new generation. Underline "had been slain," and note: *Perfect tense; permanent effect of Jesus' death.*

Observe that though the Lamb had been slain, it was standing. "Standing" is a tense form (perfect) which pictures the Lamb getting up and *remaining up* – a clear allusion to the resurrection of Jesus (see 1:18). Note that.

Finally, the phrase "seven Spirits of God" is almost certainly a reference to the Holy Spirit (see 1:4) and his abiding work (as suggested by the perfect tense form "sent forth" – cf. John 16:7) in revealing the message (*via* inspired men) regarding the redemptive work of the Lamb. Underline "sent forth" and note: *Compare with John 16:7.*

5:7

The Lamb *took* (and kept – as indicated by the perfect tense) the prophetic scroll from the Father's hand. Our Lord Jesus Christ holds the future in his hand! This is a powerful point.

5:8

The heavenly creatures fell down before the Lamb. Clearly the Lamb is shown to be superior to the living creatures and the elders. This is testimony to the divine nature of Jesus Christ (cf. Heb. 1:6). This fact is antagonistic to the "Jehovah's Witness" notion that Jesus was "nothing more than a perfect man." Underline "fell down" and note: *Christ – an object of worship.*

Notice that there is mention of harps and golden bowls full of incense. That these items are not literal is obvious. The bowls "are" the prayers of the saints. The term "are" is a metaphor, meaning "represent, symbolize." Circle "are" and enter that notation.

Some suggest that the harps of this passage afford justification for the use of musical instruments in Christian worship. That assertion is wrong. If, however, the argument were consistently pursued, there would be as much justification for incense-burning as for instruments. Circle both "harp" and "incense" and marginally note: *Both figures of speech.*

5:9-10

The Lamb "purchased" unto God a people from all nations. Here let us notice two points.

First, this is a reference to the *church* of the Lord (cf. Acts 20:28). Underscore "purchased," and note: *See Acts 20:28.* Can anyone possibly minimize the importance of the church, in view of this declaration?

Second, observe that the church is international in scope. This is a fulfillment of Isaiah's prophecy – "all nations shall flow unto it" (Isa. 2:2).

Consider also that these people "reign" (present tense, according to the best manuscript evidence – ASV; not future, as in KJV). They are *presently reigning*. This is contrary to the theory of premillennialism which sees Christ's reign as future. Mark "reign," and note: *Reign is present, not future.*

Chapter 6

6:1-8

In the previous chapter of Revelation, the Lamb (Christ) was seen taking the prophetic scroll from the Father's hand. In the present chapter, Jesus begins to unseal the document, and various images commence to appear.

John sees what has come to be known as "the four horsemen of the Apocalypse." Four horses come forth – white, red, black, and pale. It is generally agreed that these visions represent certain historical periods, to be characterized by military conquest, horrible bloodshed, famine, and finally widespread death. As to exactly when these historical events occur will depend upon how one views the thrust of the book as a whole.

Perhaps the main point that should be made is this. This context clearly indicates that God is in control of these historical events. The horsemen depicted are instruments of divine judgment, and that is indicated by the multiple use of the expression "was given" (vss. 2, 4, 8).

One scholar has noted: "The release of these four horsemen unveils to believers the fact that all the great forces of history are definitely related to Christ's permissive will" (Jones, p. 34).

And so, underline "was given" in the verses cited above, and marginally note: *God is in control.* This is a most comforting thought to Christians.

6:9

When Jesus opened the fifth seal of the scroll, John was permitted to view the souls of the martyrs underneath the altar of God. There are several points which must be made here.

First, these martyred saints are beneath the "altar." The altar (borrowed from Old Testament imagery) was an instrument of sacrifice during the Mosaic economy, and sacrificial blood was poured out at the base thereof (Lev. 4:7). The picture here is likely that of viewing slain Christians as victims of sacrifice. Perhaps it suggests, as Paul had earlier indicated, that these ancient brethren had enjoyed "fellowship" with the Lord in his sufferings (see Phil. 3:10; cf. 2 Tim. 4:6). Underline "altar" and reference these passages.

Second, the participle, "having been slain," in the original language is a perfect tense form. It thus suggests the abiding result (that of blessing) that attended their noble deaths. Mark that form, and observe: *The abiding effects of martyrdom.*

Third, one must note the cause of the deaths of these brave Christians. They died "for the word of God, and for the testimony which they held" (cf. 1:9). Their testimony was the "word of God," not the word of men. God has spoken!

Moreover, the text says "they held" that testimony. The Greek tense is an imperfect form; they kept on holding to their testimony. Note that.

They tightly clutched their faith. What wonderful examples they continue to provide to this very day. Does this mean anything in our time when some brethren are prone to throw up their hands in despair for trivial causes?

6:10

The martyrs "cried out" with a great voice. What does this imply? Though they have been killed, they are still alive – and conscious – in the spirit realm. Make that notation marginally.

Additionally, they asked: "How long, O Master?" This question indicates that their knowledge is still limited; they have not become deity (thus, omniscient), as some cultists allege will be the case for glorified saints. This is an important point. Underline "How long?" and record: *Not omniscient; not deity.*

God is designated as "Master." The Greek word is *despotes*, and it reflects "absolute and unlimited authority." The term is applied both to God (Luke 2:29; Acts 4:24) and to Christ (2 Pet. 2:1; Jude 4). From the earthly viewpoint, it must have appeared as if the Roman powers were in control; these brethren knew otherwise!

The martyrs wanted to know how long it would be before their blood would be avenged, i.e., their persecutors punished. There are two matters that should be given consideration in connection with this question. First, these saints recognized that justice demands that evil be punished ultimately. The basis for their position, as implied by the question, is in the very nature of God himself. It is precisely due to the fact that God is "holy and true" that wicked men must finally be punished. Make a notation to the effect: *Final rewards grounded in the nature of God.*

Second, comment must be made regarding the attitude of these departed brethren. Some have suggested that their disposition – petitioning for vengeance upon their adversaries – is wholly inconsistent with the exalted principles of Christianity. Such a view, however, fails to take into consideration some important information. These saints had been condemned in the court of heathen opinion and brutally executed. In this narrative, they are appealing their case to the Supreme Court for the vindication of their righteous cause. The comments of William Hendriksen are excellent: "[T]hese martyrs do not invoke retribution for their own sake but for God's sake. These saints have been slaughtered because they place their trust and confidence in God. In slaughtering them, the world has scorned him!" (p. 128). Yes, God will avenge his elect (Luke 18:7). Note these points.

Chapter 7

7:1

This chapter begins with a vision of four angels standing at the four corners of the earth. Here we are reminded of a truth so prominently portrayed in the Scriptures; angels are heavenly beings employed by God for the implementation of the divine purpose on earth. Though they are not visible today (as in Bible times – cf. Acts 10:3), nonetheless they are still operative (cf. Heb. 1:14). Underline "angels" and note: *Ministering agents of God (Heb. 1:14).*

Too, observe that the expression "four corners of the earth" represents figurative terminology which suggests the concept of universality. This is not an antiquated geographical mistake.

7:2-3

The angels of God were poised to inflict great damage upon this planet when suddenly they were restrained. Another messenger of God appeared and said, "Hurt not," i.e., do not start (so the force of the original) to hurt yet. This angel had the "seal" of God with him, which, symbolically speaking, was to be placed upon the foreheads of those who are servants of God. Mark "seal" and note: *Sign of authentication*.

Observe also that the earth was temporarily spared because of God's people (cf. Matt. 24:22). Christians are a blessing to society in more ways than the human eye can behold.

7:4-8

The number of those who were sealed (perfect tense, suggesting that the effect of the sealing remained) was 144,000. As we have indicated previously, Revelation is highly symbolic (1:1), and so it is subject to great abuse. The "Jehovah's Witnesses" argue that this chapter, together with chapter 14, prove that only 144,000 people will be in heaven (*Let God Be True*, p. 113).

Who is this group of 144,000? Some conservative scholars believe it signifies the redeemed who are out of the physical nation of Israel (Hinds, 112). Others think the number symbolizes spiritual Israel, the church (J.W. Roberts, p. 71). Be that as it may, it is generally acknowledged that the number is figurative.

That 144,000 is a symbolic number is clear from the following facts: (a) If the 144,000 were literal, the "tribes" would have to be as well. This would then exclude the patriarchs (e.g., Abraham) from heaven, for he was not from any "tribe" of Israel. Yet,

Abraham will be in heaven (Matt. 8:11). (b) Neither Ephraim nor Dan is listed; and yet, there is mention of the "tribe of Joseph" (which, actually, was not a tribe). Clearly, then, these tribes, along with their tabulated total, reflect a symbolic description. Robert Mounce comments that the 12 tribes are squared and multiplied by 1,000, which is "a twofold way of emphasizing completeness" (p. 168). Make some notes to this effect in your margin.

7:9

Apart from the 144,000, John saw a great, numberless multitude. This is proof positive that the number 144,000 is figurative. If the 144,000 represent those converted out of old Israel, the number is obviously expanded by the "great multitude." If the 144,000 and the "great multitude" signify the same group – merely from different angles (as some allege), then the 144,000 must be figurative; it cannot be a literal 144,000 and "numberless" at the same time.

The Watchtower folks claim that the "great multitude" represents the "earth class," who will live on this glorified globe forever. That is not the case, however. The great multitude is "standing before the throne," and that throne is in the temple of God, which is in heaven (see vs. 15; cf. 11:19). Underline "before the throne," and enter these references.

This multitude is arrayed in white robes. As we have observed previously, "white" is employed in this book to denote purity (3:18; 4:4), and victory (2:17; 3:4). Enter a couple of these illustrative references in your margin. For a further consideration of this matter, see "White" in Chapter 2. The "palm" branches likely signify the festive joy of those within the heavenly city (cf. John 12:13). Circle "palm," and note: *See John 12:13.*

7:13-14

Though it is not explicitly stated, the narrative implies (and we must infer) that John wanted to know the identity of the multitude. And so he was told that these are they that have come out of "the great tribulation." This is simply a general reference to the persecution they had endured – the lot of every believer, to a greater or lesser degree (see John 16:33). There is utterly no evidence that the expression denotes a specific seven-year Tribulation Period, as advocated by premillennial dispensationalists. Underline "great tribulation," and note: *General persecution.*

It is of considerable interest that this multitude had "washed their robes, and made them white in the blood of the Lamb." When were they washed? Obviously at the point of their conversion. Ananias instructed Saul: "[A]rise, and be baptized, and wash away your sins" (Acts 22:16). While we must always emphasize that our sins are purged by the Lord's blood, we can never neglect to teach how that is accomplished. Make a note to this effect.

Chapter 8

8:1-2

The eighth chapter of Revelation begins with the record of the Lamb opening the seventh seal of the divine scroll. The seventh seal consists of a scene in which a series of seven trumpets are progressively sounded. These trumpets herald impending judgments which will be visited upon the earth and the wicked enemies of God's people, thus showing the righteousness of the Creator, and his concern for his people. The vision culminates with a preview of the final judgment (11:18). The narrative affirms dramatically that sin will be punished.

In your margin, beside verse one, draw an arrow pointing down the page. Note: *Judgments to come – 8:1-11:18; vindication of saints.*

Chapter 8 deals with the blowing of the first four trumpets. The seven angels standing before the throne suggest the implementation of Heaven's will upon the earth – in a complete fashion (as reflected by the number "seven"). God still is in charge of earth's events, in spite of the fact that men deny such.

The "trumpet" takes its rise from Old Testament imagery. It was suggestive of divine intervention (Ex. 19:16, 19), and was sometimes used to signify coming judgment (see Joel 2:1f). The figure is also employed in connection with the final judgment at the end of time (1 Cor. 15:52; 1 Thes. 4:16). Circle "trumpet" and note: *Symbol of judgment.*

8:3-5

The heavenly scene is reminiscent of the tabernacle motif. Another angel came and stood over the altar. Some would identify this angel as Christ, but the term "another" (*allos*, another of the same kind) would appear to eliminate that idea. The altar is the golden altar of incense that stood just before the veil which separated the holy place from the holy of holies (Ex. 30:1-10). Earlier, the incense was representative of the prayers of the saints (5:8); here, incense is "add[ed] to" (ASV), or "mingle[d] with" (RSV) those prayers. Hendriksen speculates that the angel, who "was given" the incense may be a representative of Christ, who, as our high priest, was making intercession in heaven (p. 142). Note this possibility.

Does God really listen to the prayers of his people? Some of those early Christians, literally bathed in their own blood, must have wondered at times. This context, though, explicitly states that "the prayers of the saints went up before God." Make a note in your margin: *God listens to his people.*

The angel then takes fire from the altar and casts it upon the earth. Mounce has an interesting comment: "The prayers of the saints play an essential part in bringing the judgment of God upon the earth and its inhabitants. The martyrs' pleas in 6:10 ('How long, O Master, the holy and true, dost thou not judge and avenge our blood on them that dwell on the earth?') is here answered in part" (p. 182). Bracket verse 5 and in your margin comment: *Prayer answered; see 6:10.*

8:7

The first trumpet unleashed a judgment reminiscent of the seventh plague of Israel's exodus from Egypt (Ex. 9:13-35). As the ancient plague came upon Egypt as a consequence of rebellion, so the analogy here would suggest a similar thought. Note in your margin: *The high price of sin; see Exodus 9:13ff.*

Observe also that the destruction is only partial; this is doubtless a divine concession to initiate repentance. Will men listen? Underscore "third" and make a note: *Partial punishment leaves room for repentance.*

8:8-9

The second judgment is described as a great burning mountain being cast into the sea. The picture may come from the Old Testament where such imagery depicts great upheaval (Psa. 46:2; Isa. 54:10; Ezek 38:20).

It is worthy of note that Mt. Vesuvius had erupted and destroyed Pompey less that two decades prior to John's writing. Could this have provided some of the drama for this figure of the burning mountain? As the sea partially turns to blood, and sea-creatures die, one is reminded of the Egyptian plague where the Nile is turned to blood (Ex. 7:20, 21). Make a note on that. Jonah once sought to run from God by striking out on a sea-voyage; this destruction of the sea may suggest that one cannot escape divine judgment.

8:10-11

In the Old Testament, when God blessed, bitter waters turned sweet (Ex. 15:23-25). Here, a flaming star falls into the waters and they become bitter. This represents a judgment from heaven. Jeremiah used "wormwood" as a symbol of suffering which results from wickedness (9:15; 23:15; Lam. 3:19). Underline that term and note: *Plague from God due to sin.*

8:12-13

The fourth trumpet brings darkness, just as with the ninth plague in Egypt (Ex. 10:21f). These judgments, like the exodus plagues, are the result of sin. They may also hint of the impending deliverance of God's people (see Pack). An eagle (not angel, KJV), a bird of prey (Mt. 24:28), appears and announces a series of "woes," suggestive of three plagues yet to come. "Woe" is an interjection of warning. God will not tolerate sin forever. Underline the "woes" and note: *God's call to repentance.*

Chapter 9

9:1-4

The 9th chapter of Revelation opens with a vision of another series of devastating calamities that are to be visited upon the earth as a result of evil, and as an expression of the justice of God.

The judgments are represented as three "woes" (cf. 8:13; 9:12). "Woe" is an interjection of warning. John sees a fallen "star" who has been "given" the key to open the pit. "Star" signifies a force (frequently a national force) employed to implement divine judgment (cf. Isa. 14:12). The fact that this star "was given" the key of the abyss suggests he is operating by divine permission (cf. 6:2ff). Make notes to this effect.

From the abyss came billowing smoke and out of the smoke appeared a vast swarm of locusts. Locusts frequently represent a plague from heaven (cf. Ex. 10:1ff; Joel 1:2ff). This swarm of locusts inflicts intense suffering upon those who have not the "seal of God on their foreheads." The "seal" identifies those who belong to God (see 7:2-4; 2 Tim. 2:19). Circle the term "seal" and enter these passages.

The fact that the seal is upon the forehead may suggest that mental assent or personal conviction is required to become a Christian. It is clear that this punishment is sent from God upon those who are the enemies of his people.

9:5-10

The torment inflicted by the locusts is of a temporal nature. This is indicated by the fact that it is only for "five months," a figure of speech for limited duration (cf. 2:10). The agony of the victims is such, however, that they will wish to die, but "death flees from them." Here is a principle worth noting: there is a suffering that is worse than physical death (cf. Heb. 10:29). Again it must be observed that this fierce army of scorpion-like locusts represents a harsh punishment from God. Bracket off this section and make that marginal notation.

9:11

This avenging force operates under an "angel" (messenger) from the pit. Symbolically, the leader's name is "Destroyer," both in Hebrew and Greek. Is this an allusion to Satan? Many commentators feel that this "king" is to be identified with the "dragon" of chapter 20. If this is a reference to the devil's rule, how can this be harmonized with the concept that the judgment is from God? The point would be this: the destruction, though from God, is rendered upon those who have followed Satan as commander. Their very punishment results from heeding his diabolical influence. Bracket verse 11 and note: *Possible allusion to the consequence of following Satan.*

9:13-15

The second "woe" commences as the sixth angel (see 8:2ff) sounds his trumpet. Another temporal penalty is to be visited upon rebellious humanity. John heard a voice from the "horns of the golden altar which is before God." The golden altar is the altar of incense, which was earlier associated with the "prayers of the saints" (cf. Lk. 1:10; Rev. 5:8). It seems clear that the punishment about to be inflicted upon earth's evil ones is in response to the petitions of the saints. The Creator will avenge his elect who cry to him day and night (Lk. 18:7-8). Beside verse 13, note: *Response to prayer; see Luke 18:7-8.* How comforting these scenes must have been to persecuted Christians in those darker eras of history.

In this vision, four messengers that had been bound at the river Euphrates were loosed. The Euphrates was associated with the region from which came the chief enemies of Israel during the Old Testament era (e.g., Assyria and Babylon). God can use wicked powers to carry out his purpose in the earth (cf. Jer.

25:9-12; Hab. 1). The passage underscores Heaven's providential activity, by the use of national forces, in behalf of Christian people. Observe further that Jehovah's use of these dignitaries is precisely according to a divine schedule (vs. 15), and not as human determination would dictate. Make a note to that effect.

9:16-19

The number of this punishing force was vast – 200 million; this is the largest figure cited in the book. The apostle specifically identifies the scene as a "vision," likely to emphasize the symbolic nature of the descriptives. The destruction is horrible beyond words and seems to preview the final punishment of those who oppose the divine cause and the Lord's people. It reflects a "temporal sample" of hell.

9:20-21

One would think that men, observing these judgments which come as a consequence of evil, would repent and prepare for the final confrontation with God. Sadly, such is generally not the case. Those who do not learn the lessons of history are condemned to repeat them. And so, humanity continues in its idolatry.

The vision stresses the stupidity of serving gods that have been fashioned with human hands (cf. Deut. 4:21-28). Too, the evils that result from turning away from the true God are cataloged – murder, sorcery, fornication, theft. There is a connection between one's religious practice and his conduct. Make a marginal note: *Belief and conduct are related.*

Chapter 10

10:1

Revelation 10:1-11:13 represents an interlude between the sounding of the sixth and seventh trumpets (the trumpets reflecting judgments to be visited upon the earth). As this chapter opens, John sees "another angel" descending from heaven. This angel is not Christ, as some allege, but "another" of the angelic class mentioned earlier (cf. 9:14). The Greek term for "another" is *allos* – another of the same kind; make a note to this effect.

This angel represents the Lord in executing the affairs of providence. The description of this being suggests that he is prepared to administer both justice (arrayed with a cloud) and mercy (rainbow upon his head).

10:2

Three times the angel is represented as standing both upon the land and sea (2, 5, 8), perhaps suggesting that his message relates to the entire planet. Record that possibility in your margin. In his hand is a small scroll that is open (i.e., not sealed as in 5:1). The nature of the "little book" will be discussed subsequently.

10:3-4

The angel's voice is like a lion's roar, suggesting that he speaks with the authority of God (cf. Joel 3:16). Accompanying the voice was the sound of seven thunders. John wanted to write down the message, but he was forbidden to do so. What the words of the seven thunders were no one knows, and, like Jesus' writing upon the ground (John 8:6), it must remain a mystery.

Some suggest the sound represented a voice contrary to the will of God – a feigned revelation – hence the apostle was forbidden to record it. Others see it as an indication of additional divine judgments to descend upon the earth, but which the Lord did not deem appropriate to detail at this point.

10:5-7

The strong angel raised his right hand to heaven and swore by God himself. The oath was grounded in the eternal nature of the Lord, and his work as Architect of the whole creation. There is no created thing, above or below, that does not owe its existence to God. The scope of the created realm, here described, is virtually identical to that depicted in the language of Exodus 20:11, wherein Moses affirms that the entire creation process was accomplished within a span of six days.

If one may reject the testimony of the Bible regarding the *how long* of the creation, as many do, why could they not also reject the concept of the *Who* as well? The description of God as one "who lives for ever and ever" should be especially meaningful to any saint who is staring death in the face.

The thrust of the angel's oath would seem to suggest that when Heaven's redemptive purposes, as revealed in the "good tidings" (i.e. the gospel) are "finished," ultimate judgment will be delayed no longer. Then, the seventh angel will sound the trumpet, which event will occur in conjunction with Christ's return (see 11:15). This should encourage patience on the part of Christian people. Bracket verse 7 and perhaps note: *Consummation of gospel age at Judgment Day*.

10:8-10

John is instructed to approach the angel and take the opened scroll from his hand. The apostle went to the messenger and asked for the book. He was then told to take the scroll and eat it up. In his mouth it would taste as sweet as honey, but when it reached his stomach, it would be very bitter. What was the little scroll?

Some see the "little book" as referring merely to a specific and limited message within the Apocalypse as a whole, e.g., 11:1-13 (F.F. Bruce). Others feel that the open scroll represents the gospel (Hendriksen), or the New Testament (Coffman).

The Word of God is sometimes described as being as sweet as honey (Psa. 119:103; Jer. 15:16). It is not difficult to see, in view of the wondrous blessings which result from a submission to the Scriptures, why it should be designated as a volume of sweetness.

But why would it be described as becoming bitter? Various views have been offered. Some suggest that the sweetness is to those who obey it, while bitterness (judgment) comes to those who disobey. While it is a fact that the Word of God both blesses and judges (cf. John 12:48), what would this have to do with bitterness in John's belly? It could be the case, I suppose, that the positive proclamation of the gospel's grace would be a sweet labor, whereas the rebukes and warnings – so essential to balanced teaching – are a bitter aspect to proclaiming the truth. But there is also another possibility. It could be that the sweetness has to do with gospel blessings received, whereas the bitterness is associated with the persecution that results from living and teaching it. This view would seem to fit the context. You may wish to underline "bitter" and note: *Persecution resulting from teaching*.

10:11

The chapter concludes with a reference to the relationship of divine prophecy to the nations. The sense is either that John must proclaim the Lord's message "over" the nations – a commission.

Or else, he will prophesy "concerning" the nations – a preview of coming events. Most scholars incline to the latter view.

Chapter 11

11:1-2

The chapter begins with John being "given" a measuring rod that is calibrated according to a *heavenly* standard. The symbol is likely a reference to the divine rule of conduct, the New Testament. The apostle is instructed to measure the temple, the altar and the worshipers. This cannot refer to the Jewish temple, for it had been destroyed more than twenty years before this book was written. The temple is a symbol of the church (cf. 1 Cor. 3:16; Eph. 2:21-22). Note this in your margin.

Those who compose the church, and the worship they render, must conform to the word of God (2 Tim. 3:16-17). The imagery seems to suggest a time when the church has drifted away from the divine pattern and needs to be brought back into harmony with the Bible. Nothing may be practiced in the name of Christianity unless it conforms to the rule of the Scriptures. Make a notation to this effect.

The outer court (which was not to be measured) probably signifies the people of the world who have no regard for the authority of God's rule of faith and practice. This does not suggest that the world is not amenable to divine law. The church is again viewed under the figure of "the holy city." It is to be trodden under foot (i.e., persecuted) for forty-two months. Some see this as an indefinite period of time. Many of the reformers thought it reflected an era of bitter persecution (e.g., the Dark Ages) roughly equivalent to 1,260 years (cf. Dan. 7:25; Rev. 11:3; 12:6,14).

11:3-6

During this same historical period, God's "two witnesses" prophesy in sackcloth (i.e., under extreme difficulty). It is likely that the witnesses suggest the proclamation of divine truth. The numeral two may hint of: the two testaments (Hinds), Christ and the church (Coffman), Christ and the apostles (Winters). There is little practical difference in the foregoing. The witnesses are also said to be two olive trees and two candlesticks. This symbol is employed in the Old Testament for the word of the Lord (Zech. 4:1-6). Enter this reference in your margin.

Those who are reckless enough to oppose these witnesses do so at their own peril. Destruction will be their end (cf. 2 Thes. 2:8; Rev. 19:15). Reference these verses. The power of the witnesses is reminiscent of the wonders of the Lord's word in Old Testament history (e.g., during the days of Elijah and during the time of Israel's exodus from Egypt).

11:7-9

After the witnesses have completed their testimony under "sackcloth" conditions (v. 3), the beast ascends from the bottomless pit (obviously a Satanic force) and attacks them. For all practical purposes, they are dead. Their corpses lie in the street of "the great city" which is given three descriptives – Sodom, Egypt, and the place "where the Lord was crucified." The symbols represent wickedness, bondage, and bitter opposition.

The bodies lie in death for three and one-half days – a brief period of time compared to their 1,260 days of testimony. Truth crushed to the ground will rise again!

11:10-11

As the two witnesses are resurrected, truth is proclaimed

again, and the tables are turned. The two "prophets" torment the evil ones who dwell on the earth and these wicked enemies were in great fear. How does sacred truth torment? By rebuking vice, exposing error and predicting judgment.

11:12

The two living witnesses were invited into heaven and their enemies beheld the wonder of the event. This symbolizes the ultimate victory of truth over error. It is consistent with the general theme of "overcoming," which is so much a part of this book. Make a note to this effect.

11:13

This passage represents divine judgment being visited upon a wicked earth. Those not destroyed "gave glory to God." This does not represent a world-wide conversion of the lost. It likely suggests that divine terror will bring many to their knees in awe of God's power (cf. Rom. 14:11).

11:15

Heavenly voices declare victory as the kingdom of the world becomes the kingdom of God and his Son. Observe that the Lord reigns "forever." This cannot be a reference to an alleged earthly reign of Christ from Jerusalem, for that is supposed to last only one thousand years!

11:17-18

Note the descriptives of the Father: He is Lord (authority), God (Deity as to nature), the Almighty (limitless power) who reigns (sovereignty). Make appropriate notations.

Let the nations be angry. They will be no match for the just judgment of Jehovah. Observe that the "dead" receive their rewards. Death is not the termination of human existence. Those rewarded are those who have "feared" (revered) the Creator and "served" him. The "destruction" of the wicked suggested here is not annihilation. It is eternal, conscious torment (cf. 14:10-11). Note that the wicked have "destroyed" the earth, i.e., they have opposed the very purpose for which the planet was made.

Chapter 12

12:1-2

The chapter begins with a vision of a woman, gloriously arrayed with the heavenly luminaries. The "woman" doubtless signifies the church. The sun, moon and stars may suggest the manner in which this divine organism is viewed by God (wondrously) in contrast to the hateful way she is to be treated by Satan and his servants; or, the luminaries may hint of the light which the church emits in this world of darkness (cf. Phil. 2:15). The woman cries in "pain," which betokens the persecution to which she will be subjected.

12:3

John sees a "great red dragon" which represents Satan (v. 9), and the color red likely denotes the bloodshed which he will effect in his opposition to the cause of Christ. His designation as "the old serpent" alludes to the temptation account in Genesis 3. Clearly, John considers that record as actual history. The seven heads and ten horns possibly suggest the plenitude of power which he would diabolically exercise against the Lord's people.

12:5

The woman gave birth to a man-child who was a particular object of the dragon's wrath. Who is the man-child? Some suggest that it represents Christians collectively (Winters), i.e., the increase of the church (Hinds). Others contend that the child is Christ himself. This is principally based upon the fact that (1) the language of the Messianic psalm is applied to him (cf. 2:27; Ps. 2:9), (2) the child is caught up unto God and unto his throne.

But how could the church be said to give birth to Christ? The thought suggested could be that the church is the human instrument by which Christ is delivered to the world (Jones). Whatever the significance of the details, the general picture is plain. Satan is the bloodthirsty enemy of the Son of God and his church.

12:6

Though the dragon would have murdered the woman had he been able, God prepared a protective place for her "in the wilderness." Wilderness is sometimes used for a place of safety (cf. 1 Sam. 23:14-15; 1 Kgs. 19:4). The Lord will protect his church (cf. Dan. 2:44). Depending on one's interpretative philosophy regarding the book as a whole, the 1,260 days could signify the entirety of the gospel dispensation (Jones), an indefinite period of time (Summers), or a particular period of history roughly equivalent to 1,260 years (Barnes). The main point is that *the faithful will be cared for by God.*

12:7

The war between Michael and his angels, and the dragon and his angels is but a symbol of the conflict between Satan and the church. There is no direct allusion to any heavenly warfare generations ago (though such a circumstance could conceivably have provided the basis for the figure). The defeat of Satan and his henchmen is graphically portrayed. Note: *Satan defeated.*

12:10

The verse commences a song celebrating the fact that Satan is vanquished. Note the curious expression: "Now is come ... the kingdom." Does this indicate that the kingdom had not previously existed? No, for chapter one makes clear the present existence of Christ's kingdom. The sense is this: *The kingdom prevails over the opposition.*

12:11

The passage again focuses upon the theme of this book – *overcoming* (used seventeen times altogether). Three important points are made here. The saints can overcome because of (1) the efficacy of the Lamb's blood, (2) the message they faithfully proclaim regarding the Redeemer's mission, (3) the uncompromising loyalty they possess – even to the point of death. Underscore these significant facts. We are again reminded of the monumental fact that the mission and message of Jesus Christ is so authentic that one must not deny it – even in the face of martyrdom.

12:15

A mighty stream of water which the serpent "cast out of his mouth" would sweep away the woman were it not for divine assistance. What is that stream? It is obviously a malevolent force (cf. Ps. 18:16; Jer. 47:2). Since it derives from Satan's *mouth*, it may allude to the incessant river of lies that he instigates, and by which multitudes are deceived, e.g., atheism, materialism, modernism, Catholicism, Protestantism, etc. A truth that seems to have escaped many religious people is the fact that it is as dangerous to *believe* a lie as to speak one (cf. 1 Kgs. 13:18; Jer. 23:32; 2 Thes. 2:10-12).

12:17

This passage contains an excellent definition of what constitutes the true "seed" of spiritual Israel. The seed are those who "keep the commandments" and "hold the testimony of Jesus." In the original language, both terms are present tense participles which suggest *persistent* activity. For a companion context see Galatians 3:26-29. Circle "seed" and connect this word with "keep" and "hold" and note: *Nature of true seed.*

Chapter 13

13:1a

The previous chapter ends with the dragon (Satan, cf. 12:9) making war against those who keep the commandments of God, i.e., Christians. This chapter commences with the dragon standing by the sea, from whence arises the first of two persecuting beasts. Clearly this association is designed to show that these hateful forces are agencies of the devil. Note the connection between the chapters.

13:1b-2

The first beast is a conglomerate – leopard, bear, lion – with multiple heads and horns. Almost every scholar who has ever written on Revelation has called attention to the similarity between this image and those conveyed in Daniel 7. It is the general consensus of commentators, both ancient and modern, that this beast represents the persecuting force of the pagan Roman Empire. Ancient Rome was a militant opponent of the Christian way. Note this.

13:8

This passage mentions those whose names were not written, from the foundation of the world, in the Lamb's book of life (cf. ASV), and therefore implies that certain names *were* so written. This descriptive does not teach the Calvinistic doctrine of predestination. That denominational concept is in contradiction to scores of biblical texts which enjoin individual human responsibility as a condition of being saved (cf. Acts 2:38-40).

The true meaning thus appears to be: The divine plan of salvation, as implemented through the work of Jesus, was in the mind of Deity before the creation of the world (cf. Eph. 1:4; 1 Pet. 1:2). God, in his infinite omniscience, knowing the *type* of person who would be a fitting recipient of his grace, could suggest that such persons already had their names written in the Lamb's book. Elsewhere in this very document, having, or keeping one's name written in the book of life is dependent upon *personal responsibility* (cf. 3:5; 20:12ff).

Note this point. And remember this principle: *Symbolic passages must be brought into harmony with plain, literal ones – not the reverse.*

13:11

In this section John sees "another" beast rising up. The term "another" is significant. The Greek word is *allos*, which denotes another of the same general sort. In other words, this is another hostile, *persecuting* force. It is, however, of a slightly different character in that it is "like a lamb." Two thoughts could be suggested. The lamb-likeness may hint of a power that *appears* gentle and benevolent, but really is otherwise (it spoke as a dragon).

Additionally, many scholars have called attention to the fact that "lamb" is a symbol of sacrifice. Hence this figure may suggest that the text is alluding to a *religious* persecuting power. Most scholars incline to this view. Make a marginal notation reflecting this.

Millennialists argue that the reference is to "the Antichrist" who is alleged to be revealed shortly before the return of Christ (Schofield). This cannot be correct, for the dogma of millennialism itself has no basis in fact.

Some would see this beast as the "priesthood of the cult of the Roman emperor" (Beasley-Murray). Others, including this writer, feel that it represents the persecuting church-state Romish structure that evolved across the centuries and ultimately generated the reformation and restoration movements. Burton Coffman says that scholars who can write whole commentaries on the book of Revelation, and yet never see the *apostasy* from the faith as a force to be reckoned with, are afflicted with an exegetical "astigmatism."

13:14

This hateful, lamb-like power deceived many of earth's people by reason of the "signs" which he put forth. They are not genuine "signs" (or miracles), for God-given signs passed away when the New Testament was completed (cf. 1 Cor. 13:8ff; Eph. 4:8ff). Rather, these are "lying wonders" (cf. 2 Thes. 2:9). One of the traits of this malignant power, therefore, will be the claim of the miraculous. Beside verse 14, reference 2 Thes. 2:9 and note that the movement described there reflects a "falling away" from the faith (2:1ff).

13:16-18

This context contains the famous passage which describes the so-called "mark" of the beast. This is a very controversial passage, even among amillennialists. We will not discuss the various theories regarding the "mark" here. We have previously explored this in chapters 8 and 9. Here, we will simply observe:

(1) The mark is obviously symbolic. It identifies this persecuting agent. It is received on the forehead and in the right hand (cf. 14:9; 20:4). "Forehead" may denote the concept of *identification*, much like the Lord's people are said to have his name written on their foreheads (14:1; cf. 3:12). It may also suggest *mental assent*. The expression "right hand" probably conveys the idea of fellowship (cf. Gal. 2:9).

(2) The influence of this power is both extensive and malevolent. Those who refuse the evil "mark" are treated horribly – even killed.

(3) But those who *refuse* the "mark" reign with Christ, hence are victorious (20:4).

(4) Those who *accept* the "mark" will be subject to the wrath of God (14:9-10).

These last two points clearly reveal that the "mark" is not something imposed against one's will; rather, the reception of the mark signifies the *voluntary acceptance* of a false system of religion that opposes the truth of God and is hostile to the Lord's people.

Chapter 14

14:1

As the scene of this chapter opens, John sees a Lamb "standing," suggesting one who stood up and remains standing. Though this Lamb had been killed, he stood up again (cf. 5:6). With the Lamb are 144,000 souls. These are the redeemed. They were "purchased" from among men (v. 3) by the Lamb's blood (Acts 20:28). In contrast to those rebels who have the beast's name written on their foreheads (13:16), these are identified with the Father and his Son, having the divine names "written" (the tense suggests permanently) on their foreheads. This asserts that they had fully resolved to be forever associated with the divine order of things.

14:2-3

The redeemed were singing a "new song" and their voices thundered like rushing waters or harp players making loud music. Those who wrest this passage from its symbolic setting and see it as a justification for instrumental music in Christian worship are desperate indeed. The "harps" are no more literal than is the "water."

14:4

Clearly 144,000 does not represent a literal number, as alleged by the so-called Jehovah's Witnesses because: (1) these people are virgins which, if literal, would exclude men like Abraham and Peter; (2) they are males. Again, if literal, this would suggest that neither Sarah nor Mary would be in heaven. Mark these key terms.

It is significant that the 144,000 are said to "follow the Lamb everywhere he goes." This descriptive reveals the authority of the Lamb – inherent in his implied leadership – and it demonstrates the sort of dedication that is essential to being a Christian. What a challenge in these days when so many are inclined to follow their own inclination in religious matters.

14:7

This passage teaches some wonderful truths regarding God. (1) He is both Creator and Judge. John observes that the Lord made the heaven and the earth. This is an allusion to Genesis 1. The apostle did not subscribe to the baseless notion that the universe is the result of an accidental explosion (the Big Bang) billions of years ago. Rather, it was "made" which reflects design. (2) God is poised to render judgment. As sovereign Deity he has the right to hold men accountable for their earthly conduct. Additionally, because of his nature and his historical activity, the devout ought to fear (reverence), glorify and worship him. When one recognizes these traits of the Creator and Judge, worship will naturally flow from the honest person.

14:8

In the historical record of the Old Testament, Babylon was the evil nation that assaulted the people of God and took them captive (cf. 2 Kgs. 24-25). But the prophets declared that the day would come when Babylon would fall (cf. Isa. 13-14; Jer. 50-51). This imagery is here employed to depict the fact that the day was coming when the church's enemies would be overthrown, and the cause of Jesus Christ would triumph.

14:9-11

There is a severe warning here for those who would worship

the beast and receive his mark (cf. 13:11ff). This beast is a political-religious force that persecutes the cause of Christ. A positive descriptive would simply suggest that these are those who accept false teachings contrary to the word of the Lord. They are those who do not follow the Lamb. They are to be recipients of divine judgment.

The administration of heavenly justice is graphically portrayed under the figurative descriptive of God's "wrath" and "anger" which are prepared "unmixed," undiluted, in the cup of punishment. Underscore "unmixed" and note: *Full strength.* How does this passage square with the modern notion that God is too loving to punish anyone in hell?

Additionally, the mental state of the wicked, as estranged from God, is described as "torment." The word denotes a conscious suffering. This reveals that the state of the wicked is not one of annihilation. This is further evidenced by the fact that these evil ones "have no rest." Contrast that with the disposition of the faithful (v. 13). Finally, observe that the punishment of the wicked is "forever and ever," an expression denoting the absolutely *unending duration* of the painful suffering of hell.

14:13

The comfort of this verse is immeasurable. The righteous dead are blessed, i.e., *happy!* This reveals that the dead are conscious. However, only those who die "in the Lord," in Christ (cf. Gal. 3:26-27) are promised this blessing. This is a promise that the Spirit "saith." Note that this reflects the fact that the Holy Spirit is a person. The term "rest" does not suggest that the saints will be inactive in the final order of things, for they will "serve" God (22:3). Rather, "rest" denotes a cessation from earthly labor.

The word "labor" reflects a state of exhaustion, and probably hints of the persecution experienced by the faithful. All of that will be over when the saints are freed from the rigors of earth's difficulties. Note finally that this state of blessedness is the result of Christian "works." It is not that works *per se* justify. It is simply that one cannot be faithful without them (cf. Jas. 2:17-18).

Chapter 15

15:1

The apostle John saw a great and marvelous sign in heaven. There were seven angels who had seven plagues to dispense. The numeral "seven" denotes completeness. This would suggest that this vision previews the complete and final wrath of God which is to be visited upon the unrighteous. Throughout history God has implemented limited judgments upon the rebellious. The day will come, however, when his "wrath" will be "finished." *Earth's* history will be terminated. This does not contradict the fact that God's wrath will continue to be manifested in the eternal punishment of hell (cf. 14:10-11). Note that the "wrath" of God must be balanced with the "love" of God.

15:2-3a

In this remarkable scene there is a "sea of glass mingled with fire." The sea may denote the majesty of God (cf. 4:6). The "fire" may suggest that the divine nature is expressed in just *judgment;* or it may hint of the *purging* of those who stand in victory in the Lord's presence (cf. 1 Cor. 3:15). Of special interest is the group characterized as "victorious." We have frequently emphasized that this is the theme of this book. The word *nikao* (victory) is found in one form or another 17 times in this book (out of 28 in the New Testament).

The "victorious" are those who did not yield to the "beast" by receiving his "mark" (see notes on chapter 13) – in a word, they remained faithful to God. The "harps" are mere symbols of praise. They hint of the gratitude of those who have been delivered from the fate of the "beast" (along with those who serve him). To suggest that these harps in some way justify the use of mechanical instruments in Christian worship is a most egregious form of biblical perversion. As the "sea of glass" is not literal, neither are the "harps." Make a note to this effect.

The "song of Moses" is an obvious allusion to Israel's deliverance from Egypt and the great victory achieved by the Lord's people on that occasion (Ex. 15:1ff). The combining of the song of "Moses" and of "the Lamb" may suggest the ultimate victory of all God's saints – of whatever era of time.

15:3b-4

The song appears to reflect the united sentiments of the saints throughout history. God's "works" are great and marvelous. The "works" are the Lord's works of creation, providence and redemption – all sacred activity that ultimately leads to the final overthrow of evil. Jehovah's works reveal his power, wisdom and benevolence. Make a notation to this effect. The term "Lord" suggests authority; "God" signifies the nature of the Creator, and "Almighty" affirms that all things are under his control. "Almighty" is *pantokrator*, from two roots – *pan*, "all" and *krateo*, "to hold." Of the ten times this word is used in the New Testament, nine are in Revelation. It is important for all God's children to know that, regardless of external appearances, the Creator is still in control. The ways of God are said to be "righteous" and "true" (i.e., genuine). The Judge of all the earth does what is right (Gen. 18:25). Note this verse in your margin.

It may have seemed to those early saints who were being persecuted so viciously that Caesar was in charge. Wrong! God is "King of the ages" (or "nations" ASVfn.). That is, the Almighty is sovereign throughout all ages and everywhere, and he is working his plan. These expressions are repeatedly used to inspire confidence in the Lord's people, no matter how adverse their circumstances may be.

Verse 4 is an awesome passage. Some suggest that it reflects the ultimate disposition of all the faithful out of every nation to praise the Maker of all things. Others feel that the verse summarizes the disposition of all rational creatures in the final order of human events. It focuses upon the Day of Judgment. Lenski notes: "The teaching of the Scriptures is that in the end the whole universe will acknowledge the righteousness of all God's acts and verdicts." There will be no pompous claims: "Who is God? I have no fear of him." "Who shall not fear [respect] him?" Not a soul! Paul expressed this concept as follows when he states that we "shall all stand before the judgment-seat of God. For it is written, 'As I live,' saith the Lord, 'to me every knee shall bow, and every tongue shall confess to God'" (Rom. 14:10-11). In the end, the "righteous acts" of God will be manifest to all. As inspiration elsewhere states the matter: the "day of wrath" will be a "revelation of the righteous judgment of God" (Rom. 2:5). There will be no atheists then. Not one person will argue about his eternal destiny. Here is an important point. The Day of Judgment will not be to reveal to each soul his destiny (that will be known at the point of death; cf. Luke 16:22ff). It will be to vindicate the righteous actions of Almighty God.

15:5-6

Seven messengers proceed from the "temple" (God's abiding place) to render "seven plagues" – complete judgment. They are clothed with "golden girdles" similar to Christ's (see 1:13), suggesting that they are doing the Lord's bidding.

The smoke that filled the temple signified the glorious power of God (cf. Ex. 19:18). Heaven's wrath is poured out upon the rebellious – not merely upon Rome, as some would limit the passage. It is poured out upon all who have stood in opposition to the King of the universe. At this time no one is able to enter the temple, perhaps suggesting: "Once the time of final judgment has come, none can stay the hand of God" (Mounce). Divine judgment will be complete and final. Surely we should learn from this that now is the time of opportunity for being reconciled with our Maker.

Chapter 16

16:1

This chapter describes the pouring out of the seven bowls containing the wrath of God. That the "bowls" are symbolic is obvious, for a literal bowl could not contain "wrath." The numeral seven denotes the completeness of divine judgment upon an ungodly world. It is important to remember that the term "wrath" does not suggest that God is emotionally malevolent. Rather, it is simply an affirmation that his holy and just nature will express itself in retribution upon rebellious conduct. Underline "wrath" and note: *Reflection of God's justice.*

16:2

The initial wrath was poured out upon those who had the mark of the beast. As observed in the discussion of chapter 13, this "mark" represents those who have received the doctrines of Satan, in terms of both mental assent and that of fellowship. Note: *See 13:16-18.*

16:3

Notice that the manifestation of God's wrath, as evidenced in this general context, is very reminiscent of the plagues (sores, water turned to blood, etc.) visited upon ancient Egypt, that wicked power that oppressed Israel. This may be designed to show the persecuted Christians that their enemies will be overcome. Underline "became blood" and note: *Judgment upon oppressors; see Ex. 7:14ff.*

16:4-7

The section makes it clear that the judgment of God is a necessary consequence of his righteous and holy nature. The Creator is holy as to his character (cf. Hab. 1:13) and righteous (cf. Ps. 89:14) in terms of his actions. He therefore is qualified to "judge" on this basis (v. 7). Circle "righteous" and "holy" and connect these terms to "judge" in verse 5.

Observe also that the coming judgment is "pay back time" for evil men who have shed the blood of God's saints and prophets. Those who have acted in this vicious way are "worthy" of the punishment bestowed. Let wicked men cease their pathetic whining about how "unjust" eternal punishment is. Those who reject the grace of Heaven are deserving of their fate. Underline "they are worthy."

Reflect also upon how verse 6 contradicts an important doctrine of Roman Catholicism. According to Romanism, one cannot become a "saint" until he has been dead at least a half century. The enemies of Christianity, however, had "poured out the blood of the saints." Obviously, the saints had been alive on earth at the time. Make a note to that effect.

16:8-9

Judgments are rendered upon those who have blasphemed the name of God, i.e., spoken against (repudiated) his *authority*. Not even in the face of certain punishment will their stubborn hearts be broken. It is of considerable interest here that there is great stress upon the fact that many simply refuse to repent (cf. v. 11; 2:21; 9:20-21). Repentance is a change of mind that results in a modification of conduct. It is a prime requirement for holiness. Underscore the term in verses 9, 11.

16:10-11

Wrath is now poured out upon the throne of the beast (persecutor of God's people). The words "throne" and "kingdom" suggest the power that the beast had wielded. But darkness (as in the Egyptian plague - Ex. 10:21ff) settled upon it. The term "darkened" is a perfect tense participle, indicating that this judgment of darkness will be "permanent." Note that. The Almighty will have the final say!

16:12-16

The ancient city of Babylon was destroyed in 539 B.C. when the Persians diverted the Euphrates River and entered the city underneath Babylon's massive walls (cf. Isa. 44:27; Jer. 50:38; 51:36). That historical circumstance forms the backdrop for this prediction of the overthrow of God's enemies at the end of time.

Enter these Old Testament references in your margin.

John sees three evil forces gathering themselves for an epochal battle in "the war of the great day of God." The "beast" likely represents a political opponent (cf. 13:1ff), the "false prophet" is probably to be identified with the second beast (religious in character) of 13:11ff, while the "dragon" is Satan himself (12:9). Underline these and note these references.

Har Mageddon (Armageddon) is not a literal war to be fought in Palestine just prior to an alleged "rapture" of the saints, as argued by dispensational premillennialists. The term has its roots in the Old Testament. Numerous battles were fought on the plain of Megiddo in northwest Palestine. Probably the decisive victory of the Lord's people in Judges 4 provides the imagery for this prophetic description of the ultimate victory of Jehovah over his enemies on the final day of earth's history. The "great day of God" is apparently the same as "the day of God" in 2 Peter 3:12, i.e., the Day of Judgment. Note that reference. The event is associated with that moment when the Lord comes unexpectedly, like a thief (cf. Matt. 24:43-44; 1 Thes. 5:2; 2 Pet. 3:10). At this point in the book of Revelation, the forces are only gathering for the final conflict. The great war is actually described in chapter 19. For further discussion, see the author's chapter in: **Premillennialism: True or False?** (1978, Fort Worth Lectures).

In view of the final overthrow of evil, a blessing is pronounced upon the Christian who "keepeth" (the verb denotes *continual activity*) his garments, i.e., he maintains his fidelity to the Lord. Remember the key word in this book is "overcome." Vigilance must be the watchword in the saint's vocabulary.

Chapter 17

17:1

This chapter deals with the judgment which God is to render upon that persecuting force designated as the "great harlot" and "Babylon" (cf. 18). Who is this power? Some see it as ancient imperial Rome (Summers, Pack), whereas others (Alford, Barnes) identify it as the apostate church which comes into full bloom in the form of the Roman Catholic movement. Coffman makes a powerful case for the latter position, and it was the most common view until relatively modern times.

Underline "waters" and note: *See verse 15*. This represents the peoples over whom the harlot exercised her influence.

17:2-5

"Fornication" is a common figure in the Scriptures for religious apostasy (cf. Jer. 2:20-25). The church of the Middle Ages became an amalgamation of both religious and civil powers. See the imagery of the two beasts in chapter 13.

The true church had fled into "the wilderness" for protection (12:6). Now, in the same place, she possesses the character of a prostitute. Degeneration has occurred. The harlot is full of blasphemy, i.e., utterances against God (cf. Dan. 7:25; Rev. 13:5-6). As Babylon was the captor of God's people in the Old Testament era, so this malevolent force is to subjugate those who would faithfully serve Christ. Underscore "Babylon" and note the tie to Old Testament history.

17:6

The harlot was a vicious persecutor of the saints (cf. Dan. 7:21, 25; Rev. 13:7), and such a circumstance was enough to make John "wonder," i.e., to be "greatly amazed" (McCord). The apostle would hardly have been amazed at a persecution from civil Rome. That the church of Christ should turn into such a monster would be a matter of true wonder!

17:7-8

Clearly, the "beast" of these verses is associated with the "beast" of 13:1. The reader should review the notes pertaining to Revelation 13. See also chapters 8-10 in this work. Mark the word "perdition." The ultimate destiny of this hostile enemy of God is hell. For a discussion of the "book of life," see notes on 13:8.

17:9-11

The "beast" upon which the harlot sat had seven heads (v. 3) which are "mountains" or "kings" (i.e., kingdoms). In the Old Testament a mountain is frequently used as symbol of "government" (cf. Isa. 2:2-4; Dan. 2:35). Some expositors believe that these mountains represent oppressive forces that persecuted the people of God in earlier historical periods. The first five are sometimes identified with Egypt, Assyria, Babylon, Persia and Greece. The sixth mountain would be pagan Rome, and the seventh (which had not yet fully materialized) would be the papal regime (Coffman). What the "eighth" force is one can only wonder. It may be a horrendous secularistic system that will attempt to destroy every vestige of religion. The main point is that there is more persecution yet to come!

17:12-14

"Ten" denotes completeness, while "horns" reflect the concept of strength. Make a marginal comment to this effect. From

John's vantage point, a powerful persecuting movement was yet to arise, though its duration would not be so lengthy (one hour) as other historical oppressions had been. There was a "united front" to persecute Christianity. It is a sorry day when that sort of unity is achieved (cf. Luke 23:12).

Christ is again portrayed as a Lamb. Of the twenty-nine times that *arnion* is employed in the New Testament, twenty-eight of them are in this final book. The emphasis, of course, is upon the sacrificial nature of the Lord's work. Recall that the Lamb had been slain, but he stood up again by means of his resurrection (cf. 5:8). Enemies will "war" against the Lamb, but it is a losing battle. Christ will *overcome* (the key word of this book) them. How? Because he is King of kings and Lord of lords over all powers (cf. 1:5). Actually, the victory is already won. It is just "mopping up" time. Three terms are used of those who will share in the victory with the Lord: they are "called" (i.e., they have obeyed the gospel - cf. 2 Thes. 2:14); they are "chosen" (i.e., they have sought refuge "in Christ" - Eph. 1:4); they have remained "faithful" (they have not yielded to the pressures of persecution - cf. 2:10). Underline these three terms and enter appropriate notes. Also, compare this with 12:11.

17:15-18

As noted in verse 8, this sinister power that is to arise as an opponent of the harlot (perhaps crass secularism, atheism, materialism, etc.) will be a devastating force. But in so doing, this entity will be implementing the bidding of God. The Lord "put in their hearts to do his mind." The mysterious ways of providence are utterly beyond human comprehension. Nonetheless, the Bible clearly affirms this sort of divine operation. In the Old Testament, the Assyrian nation came against Israel as the instrument of divine wrath, though "he meaneth not so" (Isa. 10:7). Cyrus overthrew ancient Babylon at the Lord's bidding, though the Persian ruler did not even know the Lord (Isa. 45:4). Jehovah can use evil powers to enact his sovereign will – and then, punish the instrument (cf. Jer. 25:8,12). So, also, with the situation under present consideration. God's prophetic declarations concerning these so-called superpowers will be fulfilled. Make notes regarding these principles. The harlot exercised great authority over various national powers, but her day of doom was on the calendar somewhere.

Chapter 18

18:1-3

This chapter continued the description of the judgment that is to be visited upon "Babylon," the sinister force that subjugates the people of God. For a discussion of the identification of "Babylon," see notes on chapter 17.

A messenger of the Lord, with great authority and a mighty voice announces that Babylon "is fallen." The tense form emphasizes the certainty of the destruction of this malignant power. This type of prophetic confidence is common in biblical literature (cf. Isa. 21:9; Jer. 50:2). Note these references in your margin.

And just as ancient Babylon was destroyed by God because of her wickedness, and so became the dwelling place of wild creatures, this anti-God Babylon, a political-religious amalgamation, (a fornicating union between paganism and apostate religion – Alford) shall be similarly a victim of divine wrath.

18:4-5

Another heavenly voice beckons: "Come forth, my people, out of her..." The expression "my people" may be used in a two-fold sense. It may refer to honest souls who are *potential* children of God (cf. Acts 18:10). Or it may denote those who genuinely obeyed the truth initially, but then apostatized and resided finally in a false system. Make notes to this effect. In either case, it is clear that "fellowship" with religious error comes under divine censure. What a stinging rebuke to those of our day who allege that we ought to be broad-minded and thus tolerant of religious false doctrine!

18:6

Babylon is to be judged according to her "works." There is a great emphasis (more than twenty instances) in the book of Revelation on God's knowledge of human works – good or bad – and man's accountability for the same (cf. 2:2; 22:12). Let those who think that works have no place in the scheme of redemption be admonished.

18:7-8

The terminology of these verses is obviously borrowed from Isaiah 47:7-9 where the prophet sets forth a description of the utter destruction of ancient Babylon. Enter that reference in your margin. This writer must protest the view that sees this context as merely a prediction of the overthrow of pagan Rome. Here the apostle describes the ultimate fall of that monstrous system that resulted from the great "falling away" (2 Thes. 2:3ff). The harlot's boasting will fade to a whimper when the strong Lord God renders judgment.

18:9-20

The following section represents the sorrow of three groups who suffer loss due to the destruction of the harlot, spiritual Babylon. They are: the kings of the earth (v. 9), the merchants of the earth (v. 11), and the ship masters and mariners (v. 17). They are amazed and distressed at Babylon's fall. They are surprised because the destruction came in "one hour" (vv. 10,17,19), i.e., it was speedy, decisive. They were chagrined due to the fact that their paramour is gone! The symbolism of destruction is largely taken from Ezekiel's description of the fall of Tyre in the Old Testament (cf. Ezek. 27). Make a notation regarding this background. Surely the church of today can see how dreadful it is to form liaisons with the forces of the world.

Observe that great rejoicing is encouraged with reference to Babylon's destruction (v. 20). Some writers are very critical of this anthem of praise, suggesting that it is quite unchristian, in that it calls for a celebration of the enemy's demise. The charge is absolutely false. The text merely shows that the day will come when justice will be done, and the cause of God Almighty will be vindicated. See our comments on 6:10 for further consideration of this matter.

18:21

This passage has its background in the book of Jeremiah. In the fourth year of Zedekiah's reign, Seraiah was instructed by Jeremiah to take a scroll containing judgments against Babylon and journey to the famous city. He was to read a litany of warnings contained therein, and then tie a stone to the scroll and throw it into the Euphrates river. The fact that it would sink and not rise again was a token of the permanent destruction of that heathen city (Jer. 51:59-64). So now, in similar language, the complete overthrow of spiritual Babylon is envisioned. The great city will be found "no more" (see below). Bracket this verse and in your margin write: *Final destruction; see Jeremiah 51:9ff.*

18:22-23

A series of dramatic "no mores'" are found in this section (beginning in 21b). These are designed to stress the permanency of ungodly Babylon's destruction. The sound of mirth (as reflected in the music) will be heard "no more." The craftsmen will work "no more." The reason for the city's fall is plain. The harlot has prostituted herself to the princes of the earth and by her false teachings (designated as sorceries) the nations were deceived. Can the danger of religious error be made any more vivid? For other blessed "no mores" see 21:4-5; 22:3.

18:24

One of the reasons that divine punishment is to be visited upon this political religious hybrid beast called Babylon is that this entity had profusely shed the blood of the prophets and saints. For a commentary on this, read the history of the Dark Ages. How can anyone fail to see that the great persecutor of true Christianity is a force far beyond pagan Rome? But the day of visitation is coming. The harlot will be paid back double (v. 6).

Chapter 19

19:1-2

This chapter begins with an anthem of praise by a great multitude in heaven. These honor the Lord in language that is reminiscent of the Old Testament. "Hallelujah" signifies "praise

Jah" (i.e., Jehovah). Three things are emphasized: God is to be *glorified*, because by his *power* alone is *salvation* accomplished. Underscore these terms. While the world of unbelief criticizes God for his alleged harshness, the truth is, his judgment upon evil is the result of his *true* and *righteous* nature. Underscore "true" and "righteous," and connect them to "judgments." The praise proffered is in anticipation of the destruction that is to be visited upon the "harlot," i.e., the apostate force that corrupted earth's inhabitants by her teaching, and who persecuted the saints in the process.

19:3-5

The *eternal* nature of the harlot's punishment is depicted by smoke that ascends "for ever and ever." Make a marginal note to this effect. Contrary to the assertions of some, hell is not a temporary phenomenon. Because of his judgment upon evil, God is worthy of praise, hence, the subordinate beings of heaven fell before him and worshiped. The fact that God is still "sitting" (a participle reflecting *continuous* activity) on the "throne" reveals that he is ever in control of earth's affairs. The afflicted Christians can take courage from this fact. All of those who reverently respect God and who would be his servants are called upon to honor him.

19:6-8

John hears another thunderous voice from heaven. The Almighty (nine times in Revelation) is praised because he reigns; again, encouragement for God's people. The verb "reigns" is a form (aorist) in the original language which may sum up the success of the entire administration of the Lord. Moreover, the heavenly band rejoices and glorifies God because "the marriage of the

Lamb is come..." In what sense? Is the church not yet married to Christ? Of course it is (Rom. 7:4; Eph. 5:22ff). There is another sense in which there is a "final consummation" between Christ and his bride (Alford). This will occur when the Lord ultimately receives the church unto himself at the end of time (cf. 21:1ff). One must remember that the same figure of speech can have varying significance in different contexts. Again we must stress that the symbol "Lamb" is employed to show that by his sacrifice Jesus has become victorious. Observe that the "wife" (church) has "made herself ready." This phrase reveals that *personal* preparation is essential for all who would finally be with the Lamb. It eliminates those doctrines which contain a sort of "proxy" response to God (e.g., infant baptism, the doctrine of purgatory, and the Mormon notion of baptism for the dead). Underscore "herself" and note: *No proxy obedience.*

The reader is informed that the church "was given" the opportunity to clothe herself. The passive form of the verb indicates that salvation is ultimately a "gift" from God (cf. Rom. 6:23; Eph. 2:8). Be that as it is, it is nonetheless still true that she must exercise the initiative to "array herself" with "righteous acts" of obedience (cf. Matt. 22:11). Circle "acts" and write: *Obedience.* How does this square with the denominational notion that "works" do not relate to one's salvation? It doesn't!

19:9-10

The apostle is instructed to "write" another beatitude (the fourth of seven): "Blessed" are those bidden to the Lamb's marriage supper. Actually everyone is "bidden" in one sense; in another sense, blessedness comes only to those who *accept* the invitation (cf. Matt. 22:1ff).

John fell down to worship at the feet of the heavenly messenger (probably an angel; cf. 22:8), but he was restrained and told to worship God. Only deity is worthy of worship. This being is a "fellow servant" – there is *service* to be rendered even in heaven.

19:11-21

The apostle sees a preview of the final judgment. Christ comes riding forth on a white horse – a symbol of victory. He is called Faithful and True because his life was characterized by fidelity and his words were true (cf. 3:14). His mission is to "Judge and make war." His vision is one of burning penetration (cf. 1:14), and his head is adorned with many "diadems" – the crown of regal dignity (usurped by others; cf. 12:3; 13:1).

The garment of the divine Word (i.e., Christ; cf. John 1:1, 14) is soaked ("dipped" has better textual support than "sprinkled") with blood. This is not his own blood, but the blood of his slaughtered enemies. The background for the imagery is found in Isaiah 63:1-6. Note that reference. This is a shocking scene. Let rebels beware. No criticism need be offered (as the commentator Barclay did) for the vivid imagery of the judgment of God. The redeemed, with their white garments, partake of the Lamb's victory (cf. 7:14). The King of kings judges by the word of his mouth (cf. John 12:48; 2 Thes. 2:8). Finally, carrion indulge on the flesh of fallen victims. How can men read this message and still disdain the words of Christ?

The chapter ends with an affirmation of the total victory of the Word over his enemies. The opposition leadership (both civil and religious) was "cast alive" into the hell of fire. There is no room for "non-conscious punishment" here. The "rest," i.e., the followers of the beast and false prophet, are also to be destroyed. The symbolism of punishment is different in this instance, but the destiny is the same.

Chapter 20

This is probably the most misunderstood chapter in the book – at least the most misused. The chapter consists of four major sections: The Binding of Satan (1-3); The Reign of the Saints (4-6); A Brief Era of Terror (7-10); The Final Judgment (11-15). Note these divisions in your margin.

20:1-3

A messenger of God descends from heaven to bind the dragon, the old serpent – Satan. Underscore "serpent" in Genesis 3:1 and note: *See Revelation 20:2.* There are several symbols here – key, abyss (pit), chain, dragon and thousand. Why should one of these – the 1,000 years – be singled out for a literal interpretation? Note these symbols and make a marginal note reflecting this point.

Premillennialists contend that this context provides the basis for their notion that Christ will return to the earth and reign for 1,000 years from Jerusalem, but there is nothing in this paragraph that remotely hints of it. The numeral "1,000" is found more than twenty times in the book of Revelation; *never is it employed in a literal sense.* This is no more a literal "1,000" than the one hundred and forty-four "1,000" of chapters 7 and 14. The millennialists make the same mistake as the "Jehovah's Witnesses." Note that. The "1,000" may be a symbol of *completeness*, or it may simply suggest a *long period* of time. Those who subscribe to "realized eschatology," commonly known as the Max King doctrine, allege that this "1,000 years" represents the 40-year span between the death of Christ (A.D. 30) and the destruction of Jerusalem (A.D. 70). How in the name of common sense would a "thousand" symbolize "forty"?

During this 1,000-year era Satan is said to be "bound," which, in some way, suggests that he cannot "deceive" the nations. This likely indicates that during this period the sacred Scriptures have free course. Circle "bound" and "deceive the nations no more," and connect them.

20:4-6

The "thrones" which were given unto them who had been martyred for Christ reveal that death does not end the scene for the Christian. Underline "beheaded" (v. 4a) and "lived" (v. 4b) and connect them. The dead lived! Regardless of how dismal the circumstances may appear, God is in control and his cause will triumph. Circle the term "thrones" and note: *Promise of victory.*

These victorious ones are to reign with Christ for 1,000 years. Some see this as a reference to the Christian age in general – that period between the ascension of Jesus (Acts 1) and his return to render judgment (Heb. 9:28). Others see it as a symbolic period of respite from an era of severe persecution.

The "first resurrection" does not refer to a resurrection of the righteous, just before an earthly reign of Christ, to be followed, 1,000 years later, by the resurrection of the wicked. There will be a general resurrection of the dead, which will involve, at the same time, both good and evil persons (see John 5:28-29; Acts 24:15). Note these passages in your margin beside verse 6. Some feel that the "first resurrection" is an allusion to the victors' baptism at the time they became Christians (Rom. 6:3-4; Col. 2:12). It may be more in harmony with the context, however, to conclude that this "resurrection" symbolizes a relief from a period of horrible persecution, somewhat analogous to the figurative resurrection portrayed in Ezekiel 37, which depicted Judah's release from Babylonian captivity. For further study, see chapter 12 in this work.

20:7-10

Many believe that this section hints of a last-ditch attempt by Satan to destroy the work of Christ preceding the Lord's return. It may suggest a period during which the Scriptures are either quite scarce again, or almost wholly ignored. At any rate, it is clear that Satan's effort is futile.

He and his cohorts are cast into hell eternally. The term "tormented" argues for conscious punishment. Moreover, this is the very realm to which all the unfaithful will be consigned (Matt. 25:41). Enter this reference in your margin beside 20:10.

20:11-15

This section describes the great day of judgment, which signals the end of the material universe. Judgment is universal (cf. Acts 17:31; 2 Cor. 5:10) – underline "great" and "small."

Moreover, judgment is according to what is *written*, depending upon the dispensation of one's earthly sojourn (cf. Rom. 2: 16). The dual nature of man is seen in the fact that both Hades (the spirit realm) and the grave and the sea gave up the dead ones that were in "them." Note the plural; it distinguishes the receptacle of the body from that of the soul. Too, circle the term "works," and note: *Obedience*. Let those who think that salvation is a matter of unconditional grace see the great emphasis upon "works" in this concluding book of the Bible (cf. 2:5; 3:2; 22:12).

Chapter 21

As the previous chapter contained a vision of the great Day of Judgment, it is entirely fitting that the following section contains a description of the vast blessings that await the victorious people of God.

21:1

In this first section, John sees a vision of a "new" heaven and earth. What is this? It is not, as alleged by some, a renovation of this present earthly environment. The term "new" translates the Greek term *kainos*, which denotes a newness of *quality*. The first heaven and earth, i.e., the material universe, have "passed away" (cf. Matt. 24:35; 2 Pet. 3:10-13) and the sea is no more. The "new heaven" and "new earth" represent a new realm of existence, i.e., *heaven itself*. These verses are devastating to those who claim that God will renovate the earth and heaven will be right here on this planet. Jesus drew a clear distinction between heaven and earth (see. Matt. 6:19-20). Note that.

21:2

In a mixture of figures, the victorious church is described as both a "holy city," i.e., the "new Jerusalem," and a "bride" (cf. 9-10). Elsewhere Jerusalem is depicted as a symbol of heavenly things (Gal. 4:26; Heb. 11:10; 12:22; 13:14). This glorious Jerusalem stands in obvious contrast to corrupt "Babylon" (17:5; 18:2). One writer has said that the message of Revelation as a whole is a "Tale of Two Cities." It is also a contrast between the bride and a harlot! – the pure versus the corrupt. The church/bride connection is common in the New Testament (Rom. 7:4; 2 Cor. 11:2; Eph. 5:22ff; Rev. 3:12; 19:7-8). The perfect tense suggests that the preparation has been completed, and the passive voice gives glory to God for the accomplishment. No one can abide eternally with the Creator who is not "ready." Make a notation.

21:3-7

The heavenly state is one in which God dwells with his people and is their God. Circle the "no mores" emphasized in this section. The final state of the redeemed is one in which "all things" have been made "new." Observe that the water of life is a promised gift to those who thirst for it (v. 6), who exercise their "will," and who "come" (in obedience) seeking it (22:17). Underscore these significant terms and make the connection between these contexts.

21:8

Notice that the eternal state will be characterized by the absence of certain wicked ones, whose part shall be in the lake that burns (present tense, continually) with fire and brimstone (a figure for intense suffering). There is eternal retribution for rebels.

21:9-15

This reflects a symbolic description of the heavenly city itself. The community is surrounded by a wall, great and high. This likely emphasizes the concept of security – not that there is any real threat, for God's enemies have already been dispatched to hell (20:11-15). The gates, which are ever open – hence, no threat of danger (v. 25), are inscribed with the names of the twelve tribes of Israel, while the foundations have the names of the twelve apostles. These dual "twelves" perhaps suggest the presence of God's faithful from both the Old and New Testament eras. Here is an important point. The fact that the apostles are only "twelve" (when actually there were thirteen faithful apostles), illustrates how numbers are symbolically employed in the Apocalypse. Millennialists should learn something from this.

21:16-21

The city of God is represented as a huge area with length, breadth, and height – figuratively about 1,500 miles in each direction. Coffman has shown that these dimensions could accommodate many times the earth's capacity for dwelling; this is another clue that this heavenly domain is not upon the earth.

The cubed dimensions would likely remind the serious student of the Holy of Holies, i.e., the dwelling place of God in the temple (1 Kgs. 6:20). The heavenly city is symbolically portrayed in terms of precious metal and stones of unparalleled beauty.

As one illustration of this, the term "Jasper" likely refers to our "diamond." The term *endomesis* ("building," verse 18) is found only here in the New Testament. The original word is used by Josephus to signify "that which is built in," i.e., in-laid, and so here may suggest a "diamond-studded" wall. Frank Pack has well observed that "language breaks down in endeavoring to describe the radiance, the glory, the wealth, the beauty, and the magnificence of this great city."

21:22-23

Both God and Christ become the divine sanctuary. No "temple" is required; we will worship Deity directly. Again, both God and the Lamb provide the light. One can hardly read these passages and not conclude that Christ receives divine glory along with the Father. The cultists (e.g., the Jehovah's Witnesses) who would rob Jesus of his deity are seriously in error.

21:24

The international flavor of the heavenly company is indicated. One cannot but think of such prophetic passages as Isaiah 2:2-4 and Jesus' statement that "many" from "the east and the west" would sit with the patriarchs in the kingdom of heaven (Matt. 8:11).

21:25-26

Some have suggested that the phrase "there shall be no night there" contradicts 7:15, which affirms divine service "day and night." There is no conflict. The idiomatic phrase in 7:15 merely denotes *continual* service, whereas the language of 21:25 is designed to emphasize the glory of God. Only a crude literalist would see a discrepancy.

21:27

We are again reminded that the filthy, abominable, and the untrue are excluded from the heavenly environment. Note that John declares that "anything" that is unclean will be barred from heaven. If infants are born in sin, as many denominationalists allege, and then die in that state, how could they, as "unclean" beings, be elsewhere but in hell? Yet such a concept violates many biblical truths (cf. Matt. 18:3).

Circle "anything" and note: *Argument against "infant sin."* The Lamb's book of life contains the redemptive record of all for whom he died – of every dispensation (cf. Gal. 4:4-5; Heb. 9:15). How great will be our final reward!

Chapter 22

There is a theme connection between the book of Genesis and the book of Revelation. Many things that go wrong at the commencement of human history, as revealed in the Genesis record, are shown to be rectified in the final consummation of things, as depicted in Revelation. This is wonderfully illustrated in chapter 22.

22:1-5

This first section might be aptly designated "Paradise Restored." John sees a garden that is reminiscent of Eden. From the throne of God and Christ there flows a river containing the water of life. This represents the eternal life that is available for the inhabitants of heaven. Circle the term "life" and connect it with the word "throne." "Throne" signifies the sovereign authority to bestow that life, a prerogative possessed only by deity. The fact that Christ is on the throne reveals that he has been victorious. All of the saints' needs are supplied – water (from the river of life), food (from the tree of life), and health (the leaves of the tree of life). The curse imposed in Eden is now removed, implying, for one thing, that death will be no more (cf. 21:4). Observe also that in the final abode the saints are *serving* God. Those who have not learned to love service in this life will hardly be prepared to enjoy the eternal city. The "mark" on the forehead is a symbolic suggestion that the inhabitants of heaven belong to the Lord. It may also hint that they gave mental assent to his teaching (cf. 13:17).

22:6-7

There is a divine affirmation that the words of this sacred book are "faithful and true," and that the same God who spoke through the prophets has communicated through his apostle. Despite the doubts of those like Luther – "My spirit cannot adjust itself to the book [of Revelation]" – there is ample evidence for the authenticity of this document. The fact that the scenes of Revelation are depicted as "shortly" coming to pass, accompanied by the Lord's promise, "I come quickly," have led some (e.g., the advocates of "realized eschatology") to assert that the second coming of Christ occurred in the first century, and thus all Bible prophecy has now been fulfilled. Such a view ignores the symbolic nature of *time* language in conjunction with biblical prophecy. "Time" is frequently *relative* in prophetic jargon (cf. Deut. 32:35; Obad. 15; Rom. 16:20). For a more detailed discussion of this matter, see Appendix III. Finally, underscore the admonition to "keep" the words of this book – a clear indication that this narrative is to be studied, understood and personally applied.

22:8-9

The apostle was so taken by the testimony of the angel that he fell at his feet to worship. But the heavenly messenger forbade such (cf. 19:10), admonishing: "Worship God." The fact that angels are not worthy of worship, combined with the fact that Jesus accepted such (cf. Matt. 14:33), clearly demonstrates that Christ was not an angel, as alleged by the "Jehovah's Witnesses." Make a notation to this effect. This truth is also forcefully emphasized in the opening chapter of Hebrews. Too, reflect upon this point: John's blunder is here *honestly recorded* – an indication of the impartiality, hence, the inspiration, of the narrative.

22:10-15

John is instructed not to seal up the scroll, for "the time is at hand." The dramatic scenes of this great document will *soon begin* to unfold. This does not mean, however, that the *entire* book must be fulfilled immediately. As F.F. Bruce has observed: "In the Christian doctrine of the Last Things ... the imminence of the end is moral rather than chronological; each successive Christian generation, for aught that is known to the contrary, may be the last generation. In that sense the time is always near (1:3)..." (p. 1711). Verse 11 is difficult and has been the subject of much debate. The probable meaning is: "If the unrighteous and filthy will not be warned by the words of the prophecy of this book, the final revelation of God, there is nothing more to be done" (Lenski, p. 665). The Lord will come quickly and give to each his reward. This suggests that God will honor the decision-making capacity of even the wicked, and in that state they will die. There is no room here for purgatory or any other sort of post-death redemption. Circle the term "work" and observe that, contrary to the baseless assertions of those who affirm "unconditional salvation," judgment will be based upon man's obedience.

The expressions "Alpha and Omega," etc. are terms that apply only to a divine being (cf. 1:8; 21:6), and are thus strong evidence for the deity of Christ.

A blessing is pronounced upon all who "wash their robes." (The KJV has "do his commandments." The better textual evidence tips in favor of the ASV.) Note several points. First, the mode of cleansing is by the Lamb's blood (7:14). Second, "wash" is a present tense form, which reveals that one must continually access the cleansing blood of Jesus (cf. 1 John 1:7). Third, by virtue of Christ's sacrifice, the faithful have a "right" to the tree of life. We deserve nothing on our own merit; we can claim everything because of what *he* did!

22:16

Jesus is the "root and the offspring of David." As a divine being, Christ was David's "root" (source); as a man, he was an "offspring" of the great king. Note this and in your margin write: *See Matthew 22:43ff.* There Jesus baffled the Pharisees by asking how the Messiah could be both David's *Lord* and *son*. The question can be answered only in light of Jesus' dual nature.

22:17-19

In this concluding invitation of the Bible (v. 17), several important truths are contained. First, observe that the *personality* of the Spirit is indicated. Second, note that man's *free will* is stressed. Third, consider that one will never be motivated to "come" until he becomes spiritually *thirsty*. Fourth, reflect upon the fact that though the water of life is "freely" given, one must be willing to personally *take of it*, i.e., accept the gift through obedience. Finally, let us be admonished not to tamper with divine revelation. By the side of this verse enter: *See also: Deuteronomy 4:2; Proverbs 30:6. No man should attempt to modify God's word.*

SOURCES

Alford, Henry (n.d.), *The New Testament for English Readers* (Chicago, IL: Moody Press).

Arndt, William & Gingrich, F.W. (1967), *A Greek-English Lexicon of the New Testament* (Chicago, IL: University of Chicago Press).

Attwater, Donald (1961), *A Catholic Dictionary* (New York, NY: MacMillan).

Baker, David W. (1988), *Nahum, Habakkuk, Zephaniah* (Downers Grove, IL: Inter-Varsity Press).

Baldwin, Joyce G. (1978), *Daniel* (Downers Grove, IL: Inter-Vasity Press).

Barclay, William (1957), *Letters to the Seven Churches* (Nashville, TN: Abingdon).

Barclay, Willian (1959) *The Revelation of John* (Philadelphia, PA: The Westminster Press), Vol. 2.

Barnes, Albert (1853), *Notes on the Book of Daniel* (New York, NY: Levitt & Allen).

Barnes, Albert (1954), "Revelation," *Notes on the New Testament* (Grand Rapids, MI: Baker Book House).

Barnes, Albert (1955), "Thessalonians, Timothy, Titus, Philemon," *Notes on the New Testament* (Grand Rapids, MI: Baker Book House).

Beasley-Murray, G.R. (1970), "The Revelation," *The New Bible Commentary: Revised* (Grand Rapids, MI: Eerdmans).

Blaiklock, E.M. (1980), *Blaiklock's Handbook to the Bible* (Old Tappan, NJ: Revell).

Bloomfield, S.T. (1837), *The Greek Testament With English Notes* (Boston: Perkins & Marvin), Vol. II.

Bright, Tom (1984), "Difficult Passages – V," *Studies in the Revelation,* Dub McClish, Ed. (Denton, TX: Valid Publications).

Brinsmead, Robert (1974), *Present Truth,* September.

Brown, David (1882), *Christ's Second Coming – Will It Be Premillennial?* (Edinburgh: T. & T. Clark).

Bruce, (1979), *The New Layman's Bible Commentary*, Eds. G.C.D. Howley, F.F. Bruce, H.L. Ellison (Grand Rapids: Zondervan).

Campbell, Alexander and Purcell, John B. (1914), *Debate on the Roman Catholic Religion* (Nashville, TN: McQuiddy).

Carpenter, W. Boyd (1959), "The Revelation of St. John the Divine," *Ellicott's Commentary on the Whole Bible,* C.J. Ellicott, Ed. (Grand Rapids, MI: Zondervan), Vol. VIII.

Charles, R.H. (1920), *A Critical and Exegetical Commentary on the Revelation of St. John* – International Critical Commentary (Edinburgh: T.&T. Clark).

Clarke, Adam (n.d.), "The Revelation of St. John the Divine," *Clarke's Commentaries* (Nashville, TN: Abingdon), Vol. VI.

Coffman, James Burton (1979), *Commentary on Revelation* (Abilene, TX: ACU Press).

Coffman, James Burton (1981), *Commentary on the Minor Prophets* (Austin, TX: Firm Foundation), Vol. 2.

Coffman, James Burton (1986), *1 & 2 Thessalonians, 1 & 2 Timothy, Titus, Philemon* (Abilene, TX: ACU Press).

Conway, Bertrand L. (1929), *The Question Box* (San Francisco, CA: Catholic Truth Society).

Conybeare, W.J. & Howson, J.S. (1889), *The Life and Epistles of St. Paul* (London: Longmans, Green, & Co.).

Cox, William E. (1977), *Biblical Studies in Final Things* (Nutley, NJ: Presbyterian & Reformed Publishing Co.).

Damsteegt, P.G., Editor (1988), *Seventh-day Adventists Believe* (Hagerstown, MD: Review and Herald Publishing Association).

Ellicott, C.J. (1978), *Galatians, Ephesians, I & II Thessalonians* (Minneapolis, MN: James Family Publishers).

Elliott, E.B. (1847), *Horae Apocalypticae* (London: Seeley, Burnside, & Seeley).

Eusebius (1955 Reprint), *Ecclesiastical History* (Grand Rapids, MI: Baker Book House).

Ford, J. Massyngbaerde (1992), "Millennium," *The Anchor Bible Dictionary*, David N. Freedman, Ed. (New York, NY: Doubleday), Vol. 4.

Girdlestone, Robert (1973), *Synonyms of the Old Testament* (Grand Rapids, MI: Eerdmans).

Goyau, Georges (1913), "Saint Bartholomew's Day," *The Catholic Encyclopedia* (New York, NY: Encyclopedia Press), Vol. XIIIl

Gundry, Robert (1970), *A Survey of the New Testament* (Grand Rapids: Zondervan).

Harrison, Everett F. (1964), *Introduction to the New Testament* (Grand Rapids: Eerdmans).

Hendriksen, William (1980), *More Than Conquerors* (Grand Rapids, MI: Baker Book House).

Hiebert, D.E. (1975), "Root," *Zondervan Pictorial Encyclopedia of the Bible*, Merrill Tenney, Ed. (Grand Rapids, MI: Zondervan), Vol. 5.

Hinds, John T. (1955), *A Commentary on the Book of Revelation* (Nashville, TN: Gospel Advocate Co.).

Hodge, Charles (1960), *Systematic Theology* (London: James Clarke & Co., LTD), Vol. III.

Horne, Thomas Hartwell (1841), *An Introduction to the Critical Study and Knowledge of the Holy Scriptures* (Philadelphia: J. Whetham & Son).

Hurlbut, Jesse L. (1954a), *The Story of the Christian Church* (Philadelphia, PA: Winston Co.).

Hurlbut, Jesse L. (1954b), *A Bible Atlas* (New York, NY: Rand McNally).

Jackson, Wayne (1984), "Answering False Doctrines Relating to Revelation," *Studies in the Revelation*, Dub McClish, Ed. (Denton, TX: Valid Publications).

Jackson, Wayne (1987), "Does Personal Recognition Exist Beyond Death?", *Christian Courier*, May.

Jackson, Wayne (1989), "Book of Revelation – When Written?" *Christian Courier*, November.

Jackson, Wayne (1990a), *The A.D. 70 Theory – A Review of the Max King Doctrine* (Stockton, CA: Courier Publications).

Jackson, Wayne (1990b), "Are the Dead Conscious?" *Christian Courier*, December.

Jackson, Wayne (1990c), "Daniel: A Test Case In Bible Prophecy," *Reason & Revelation*, July.

Jamieson, Robert, Fausset, A.R., Brown, Robert (1990), *A Commentary – Critical, Experimental, and Practical on the Old and New Testament* (Grand Rapids, MI: Eerdmans). Vol. One.

Johnson, Alan (1981), "Revelation," *The Expositor's Bible Commentary*, Frank Gaebelein, Ed. (Grand Rapids, MI: Zondervan), Vol. 12.

Jones, Russell Bradley (1969), *The Triumphant Christ and His Church* (Birmingham, AL: Jones).

Kelcy, Raymond (1968), *The Letters of Paul to the Thessalonians* (Austin, TX: Sweet Publishing Co.).

Kik, J. Marcellus (1948), *Matthew Twenty-Four* (Philadelphia, PA: Presbyterian and Reformed).

King, Max R. (1987), *The Cross and The Parousia of Christ* (Warren, OH: Parkman Road Church of Christ).

Ladd, George L. (1962), "Eschatology," *The New Bible Dictionary*, J.D. Douglas, Ed. (Grand Rapids, MI: Eerdmans).

Laetsch, Theo. (1956), *The Minor Prophets* (St. Louis, MO: Concordia Publishing House).

Lanier, Roy H., Sr. (1978), "Revelation 20 – An Analysis and Exegesis," *Premillennialism, True Or False?* Wendell Winkler, Ed. (Fort Worth, TX: Winkler Publications).

Lee, William (1981), "The Revelation of St. John the Divine," *The Bible Commentary*, F.C. Cook, Ed. (Grand Rapids, MI: Baker Book House).

Lenski, R.C.H. (1963), *The Interpretation of St. John's Revelation* (Minneapolis: Augsburg).

Lenski, R.C.H. (1961), *St. Paul's Epistles to the Colossians, Thessalonians, to Timothy, Titus, & Philemon* (Minneapolis: Augsburg).

Let God Be True (1946), (Brooklyn, NY: Watch Tower Bible and Tract Society).

Leupold, H.C. (1969), *Exposition of Daniel* (Grand Rapids, MI: Baker Book House).

Lindsey, Hal (1970), *The Late Great Planet Earth* (Grand Rapids, MI: Zondervan).

Manley, G.T. (1947), *The New Bible Handbook* (Chicago, IL: Inter-Varsity Press).

Mare, Harold W. (1975), "Man of Sin," *Wycliffe Bible Encyclopedia* (Chicago, IL: Moody Press), Vol. II.

Mason, A.J. (1959), "II Thessalonians," *Ellicott's Commentary on the Whole Bible,* C.J. Ellicott, Ed. (Grand Rapids, MI: Zondervan), Vol. VIII.

McGuiggan, Jim (1976), *Revelation* (Lubbock, TX: International Biblical Resources).

M'Clintock, John & Strong, James (1968), "Anti-christ," *Cyclopedia of Biblical, Ecclesiastical, and Theological Literature* (Grand Rapids, MI: Baker Book House), Vol. I.

M'Clintock, John & Strong, James (1970), "Revelation," *Cyclopedia of Biblical, Theological, & Ecclesiastical Literature* (Grand Rapids: Baker),Vol. VIII.

McCord, Hugo (1981), "The Number 666 ...", *Difficult Texts of the New Testament Explained,* Wendell Winkler, Ed. (Hurst, TX: Winkler Publications).

Milligan, Robert (1957), *The Scheme of Redemption* (St. Louis, MO: The Bethany Press).

Milligan, W.W. (1903), "The Book of Revelation," *An Exposition of the Bible* (Hartford, CN: S.S. Scranton Co.), Vol. VI.

Morris, Leon (1980), *The Revelation of St. John – Tyndale New Testament Commentaries* (Grand Rapids, MI: Eerdmans).

Mounce, Robert H. (1977), *The Book of Revelation* (Grand Rapids, MI: Eerdmans).

Murray, George L. (1948), *Millennial Studies* (Grand Rapids, MI: Baker Book House).

Nestle, Eberhard (1899), "Har-Magedon," *A Dictionary of the Bible, James Hastings*, Ed. (Edinburgh: T. & T. Clark), Vol. II.

Newton, Thomas (1831), *Dissertations on the Prophecies* (London: Blake).

Orr, James (1939), *The International Standard Bible Encyclopedia*, James Orr, Ed., (Grand Rapids: Eerdmans).

Pack, Frank (1984), *The Message of the New Testament – The Revelation* (Abilene, TX: Biblical Research Press), Vol. I & II.

Pentecost, Dwight (1985), "Daniel," *The Bible Knowledge Commentary*, Roy Zuck, Ed. (Wheaton, IL: Victor Books), Vol. I.

Plumptre, E.H. (1891), *Epistles to the Seven Churches* (London: Hodder & Stoughton).

Pohle, J. (1913), "Toleration," *The Catholic Encyclopedia* (New York, NY: Encyclopedia Press), Vol. XIV.

Richards, Lawrence P., Editor (1990), *The Revell Bible Dictionary* (Old Tappan, NJ: Fleming H. Revell Co.).

Roberts, J.W. (1974), *The Revelation To John* (Austin, TX: Sweet Publishing Co.).

Robertson, A.T. (1925), *An Introduction to the Textual Criticism of the New Testament* (Nashville: Broadman).

Robertson, A.T. (1933), *Word Pictures in the New Testament* (Nashville: Broadman).

Rose, H.J., and Fuller, J.M. (1981), "Daniel," *The Bible Commentary*, F.C. Cook, Ed. (Grand Rapids, MI: Eerdmans), Vol. VI.

Salmon, George (1904), *An Historical Introduction to the Study of the Books of the New Testament* (London: John Murray).

Sanderson, Edgar, Lamberton, J.P., McGovern, John (1900), *The World's History and Its Makers* (Chicago, IL: Universal History Publishing Co.), Vol. I.

Schaff, Phillip (1980), *History of the Christian Church* (Grand Rapids, MI: Eerdmans), Vol. I.

Schaff, Phillip & Jackson, Samuel (1894), *A Religious Encyclopedia – Biblical, Historical, Doctrinal, and Practical Theology* (New York: Funk & Wagnalls).

Scofield, C.I. (1909), *The Scofield Reference Bible* (New York, NY: Oxford University Press).

Shank, Robert (1982), *Until – The Coming of Messiah and His Kingdom* (Springfield, MO: Westcott).

Sheriffs, R.J.A. (1962), "Har-Magedon," *The New Bible Dictionary*, J.D. Douglas, Ed. (Grand Rapids, MI: Eerdmans).

Smith, Wilbur (1963), "Revelation," *The Wycliffe Bible Commentary*, Charles Pfeiffer & Everett Harrison, Eds. (London: Oliphants).

Smith, William Taylor (1939), "Number," *The International Standard Bible Encyclopedia*, James Orr, Ed. (Grand Rapids, MI: Eerdmans), Vol. IV.

Strauss, James D. (1963), *The Seer, The Savior, And The Saved* (Joplin, MO: College Press).

Stone, Nathan (1944), *Names of God* (Chicago: Moody).

Thayer, J.H. (1958), *Greek-English Lexicon of the New Testament* (Edinburgh: T.&T. Clark).

Thiessen, H.C. (1943), *Introduction to the New Testament* (Grand Rapids, MI: Eerdmans).

Thiessen, H.C. (1949), *Lectures in Systematic Theology* (Grand Rapids, MI: Eerdmans).

Vine, W.E. (1991), *Vine's Amplified Expository Dictionary of New Testament Words* (Iowa Falls, IA: World Bible Publishers).

Vos, Geerhardus (1939), "Eschatology of the New Testament," *International Standard Bible Encyclopedia*, James Orr, Ed. (Grand Rapids, MI: Eerdmans).

Wilder, John B. (1959), *The Other Side of Rome* (Grand Rapids, MI: Zondervan).

Winters, Howard (1989), *Commentary on Revelation* (Greenville, SC: Carolina Christian).

Woods, Guy N. (1964), *The Epistle of James* (Nashville, TN: Gospel Advocate Co.).

Workman, Gary (1988), "Who is the man of sin?" *Studies in 1 & 2 Thessalonians,* Dub McClish, Ed. (Denton, TX: Valid Publications).

Young, Edward (1980), *The Prophecy of Daniel* (Grand Rapids, MI: Eerdmans).

Zahn, Theodor (1977), *Introduction to the New Testament* (Minneapolis, MN: Klock & Klock), Vol. III.